MY TIME WITH THE DEVIL

THE DEVIL

And The Truth about Hell, Satan & Spiritual Warfare

W.E. SMITH

Author: W.E. SMITH

Project manager W.E. SMITH

WillHouse Publishing LLC

This book may be purchased for educational, business, or sales promotional use. For information, kindly contact the author.

WillHousePublishing@gmail.com

Quotes from:

UCLA Professor Henry Ansgar Kelly

Catholic Answers website

Unless otherwise noted, Scripture quotations are from the King James Version (KJV), 1604, or The American Standard Version (ASV), officially Revised Version, Standard American Edition, 1901

Book Cover Art:

Licensed from Freepik.com for Unlimited Use without Attribution

CONTENTS

INTRODUCTION

Even before I reached my teens, I was a victim of horrifying demonic attacks often. I would be Physically Beaten, Tormented, and Haunted by Evil Spirits for many years. Then it all stopped. In this book, I will tell my True Story of Demonic Abuse, how I've been free from it for over a decade, and how you can be free as well. We will Uncover the truth about Hell, the true power of Death, the truth about Spiritual Warfare, all the different Biblical names of Satan, and the true Essence of Evil.

Chapter One

THE EXORCIST

For over 30 years I had been struggling with the Devil and his demons. They would regularly talk to me, they would scare me, and they would attack me. I would routinely be attacked in my bed while sleeping. They would smack me and wake me up out of my sleep. I would be knocked to the floor out of my bed and there were a few times that I felt like they were about to kill me. But let's go back to the beginning when I was a very young child. As a child, I was very brave. I was fearless. I remember grownups saying to my Mother, "Wow Shelley, your son Billy doesn't seem to be afraid of anything". At that time in my life it was only Me, my Mother, and my little Brother, so I felt like the man of the house, like I had to be the protector of the family. Fear felt like a luxury that I had no time for but that fearlessness was short-lived. One day my mom called my brother and me in from playing because she was very excited about a movie that was coming on TV that she had gone to the movie theater to see. In preparation for this movie, she had made us some rice krispie treats, some popcorn, and Kool-Aid. I remember it like it was yesterday. The movie was called, "The Exorcist" and she was very excited about it. She said it was really scary. Y'all gone be scared. She kept telling us to prepare ourselves, get ready but by this age I had learned that Mom was a fibber, she had lied to me about Santa Claus she had lied to me about the Tooth Fairy, she had lied to me about where babies came from so, to be honest with you I didn't put too much stock into moms excitement. I felt I was too old to fall for Mom's tricks again. Let me take a side note or a brief detour. I've realized the more that I've said this to people that I am in the minority in this thought but I don't believe that you should tell your children lies about Santa Claus the Tooth Fairy etc because it leads your children to not believe what you say once the truth is discovered. It seems like the mass consensus is that when you don't train your kids to believe in the fairy tales about Santa Claus, The Tooth Fairy, Easter Bunny, etc. then you're taking away their ability to dream or their imagination. I'm not certain that child psychology would agree with that premise. But in my personal experience, it seemed like it only caused me to distrust my parents, to not believe in them anymore, to think now everything they're saying was probably a lie. So maybe that didn't happen to you. Maybe it didn't affect you that way but it did me and I just can't imagine that I'm alone in this. I never wanted my kids to distrust what I said, I always wanted them to believe that what Dad said he meant and it is true. So I never lied to my children about Santa Claus or anything else but you do whatever you want to do, no big deal, that's just my little opinionated side note. Let me get back to the story. My Mom kept bragging about how scary this movie was and she was excited. I remember that, even as I'm talking about her right now, and her excitement was contagious so my brother and I were beginning to get

9

excited as well. Now we're ready to see this movie too, but as we begin watching The Exorcist the movie seems so far-fetched. There was this little girl who was small and young like us and was giving these grown-ups such a hard time.

Since then I've learned that in a lot of white homes, a little white girl or boy can wreak a bunch of havoc in a home because of the freedom they were allowed but I believe that kind of behavior was absolutely unbelievable in African American homes. Which added to my sheer disbelief in the strength or believability of this movie. I do remember thinking that her spinning her head all away around, talking in deep voices, and spitting the green stuff out of her mouth. Now that was unique and grabbed my attention because we hadn't seen anything like that before but it didn't necessarily scare me. I just thought, what is that, she was really sick. I thought it was different, unique, or imaginative. Honestly, I have to admit that I wasn't afraid. The movie wasn't scary at all and if memory serves me correctly, my little brother wasn't afraid either and this baffled my mom. She sat there just enthralled, I remember her face being shocked, just finding it unbelievable that we were not scared. Occasionally, like when the music would peek to its frightening crescendo, mom would jump at us trying to scare us and we just laughed or something like that or maybe jerked because of her catching us off guard but the movie was not scary at all. I remember my brother and I at different times were laughing during the movie which again was just surprising my mom. I remember my mom asking me, "Billy, why aren't you scared" I said, "Mom this ain't real". She swore it was real and I just knew mom was pulling the old Santa Clause on me all over again and I was determined not to fall for this fib as I had for all the others. So my mom began to try to convince my brother and I that this kind of stuff is real. She went into elaborate stories of things she experienced with demons, ghosts, witches, etc. all while growing up. I remember laughing at all the lengths my mom was going to, to try to convince my brother and me that this stuff was real I remember just laughing in my mom's face and she was so serious like really listen Billy, listen. I'm just like come on Mom cut it out, I'm not about to fall for the banana in the tailpipe again, LOL. But at the time I thought I was not falling for the tooth fairy or Santa Claus again. I'm not, I'm not falling for it, Mom! I remember my mom getting serious and just really going into all these stories and these very sad and scary things that happened to her and then she said, "You can call your aunts and uncles to verify what I'm saying." So we called her brothers and sisters right then and there on the phone and to my surprise they confirmed what she said. I remember the shock of hearing my aunt and my uncle's confirmation saying yeah this did happen. They confirmed an unbelievable story my mom told us about a man who had fire all over his body, just walking down a hallway of their childhood home moaning. I remember thinking there was no way they could have planned this. How could they have known we were about to call them about this? It was shocking and it was spooky. I began to believe what my mom was saying. Up to this point, if

I was afraid of the dark it was only because I felt like a family member might jump out and try to scare me like they would occasionally do but I wasn't afraid of the dark normally I could sleep in the dark I didn't need a nightlight or anything like that. I had absolutely no fears of the dark, no fears of demons or ghosts or monsters in the dark, until that day. My life changed almost immediately.

Chapter Two

MY TIME WITH THE DEVIL

I began to see normal things like a simple pile of clothes in the chair turn out to be somebody or something. My world started to transform, I would see something like a human figure flash past the corner of my eye, and I started hearing voices. Whenever I would go into dark places they began feeling cold and eerie like somebody was over me or coming near me all kinds of crazy things started happening. Now I was becoming Keenly aware of demons, spirits, or ghosts. My Mom got saved and started to take us to Church. I fell in love with church and I became a church boy and was going to church all the time. Then I started to hear the pastor talking about the Devil, demons, and evil spirits just confirming even more what my mom was saying. So I began to notice demons more and more. I believe I was around the age of 13 when things started getting much worse. I was asleep on the couch which was my bed at the time. My little brother had a little twin-sized bed in the other room we used to share and I was sleeping on the couch because the twin bed was too small for us both plus I could have some space from my little brother. While I was asleep on a couch I felt something slap me real hard on my face. I jumped up and began looking all around swearing my little brother had hit me in my sleep. I didn't see him or anyone so I began searching all through the closet, I was mad & ready to beat him up. I was looking all around for him, I opened my door and went all the way to the other room opening his door, and found him sleeping in the bed. I began checking him to see if he was faking, even though I believed it to be almost impossible for him to smack me, close my door and his, and get into the bed without me seeing or hearing him. I remember asking myself, how did he get past me? Is he really asleep? But he was sound asleep and I'm freaking out. Who just hit me? My door was shut, nobody was in the room but me. That was new. I remember not too long after that I was asleep on that same couch and I felt some pressure on my chest, I woke up, opened my eyes, and as soon as I opened my eyes I felt something kick me, It felt like two feet right in the middle of my chest and two feet on my side kicked me and knocked me off the couch. It was almost like somebody was on top of me and when I opened my eyes I startled them so they were shocked and jumped to flee and the force of that kicked me off the couch and totally freaked me out. I was pushed like a kick right to my side. I still remember it knocked me onto the floor and I remember thinking that something was happening, something was different, another level of attacks were coming and this was not too long after I got the smack in my face. I was also dealing with a lot of anxiety and depression and suicidal thoughts at this time I told a minister at church about what was happening to me and he said that the Devil knew I had a calling on my life so he was coming against me to try to destroy me and then he began to start telling me about spiritual warfare how I could battle with those demons to stop them from destroying me. He started telling me about talking in tongues, binding and loosing, tearing down strongholds, pleading the blood of Jesus, etc. So now I was mad realizing the Devil was trying to destroy me and that made sense because all of a sudden I was going through this anxiety and depression, I was also having these physical attacks, and things were just going bad all around me. It made sense, The Devil's trying to get me! So I went into warfare with the Devil and his demons. Whenever I felt attacked emotionally, physically, or spiritually by the Devil, it was on. I fought back now, I would go into talking in tongues, rebuking the Devil and his demons, tearing down strongholds. I would walk around in anger talking to the Devil like he was standing right in front of me. I remember at times even punching the air while I was praying and I could swear that sometimes it felt like I was hitting the demons back and I continued binding and loosing, tearing down strongholds, rebuking, spreading anointing oil all over the place for years. Spiritual warfare became an everyday thing, I began to see the Devil's handiwork in everything. I could spot him a mile away but his attacks against me seemed to get worse as I battled him in spiritual warfare. Around this time I would routinely about three times a week be awakened with a heaviness on my chest like someone was leaning on me and someone's hand was pressing up hard against my mouth so I couldn't talk and right under my nose so I could barely breathe and this horrified me because now I was aware that the Devil was attacking me and my response to his attacks was to go into spiritual warfare but it seemed like the demons got wise to my weapon of defense so now they were holding my mouth so I couldn't even speak against them. I couldn't battle them with the name of Jesus, with the Scriptures or my words, I couldn't talk in tongues, I couldn't plead the blood, I couldn't rebuke, bind, or loose because I could not speak. And because I couldn't bind, loose, rebuke, or talk tongues, this pressure, this holding my mouth lasted way longer than normal almost like they were choking to suffocate me and I couldn't do anything to stop them. I'd try to mumble and rebuke the Devil under my breath. This frightened me. It was as if the demons got smarter, they knew that I would battle them, that I would go into spiritual warfare with them so they held my mouth to shut him up. It made me feel helpless, this went on for years. Sometimes I'd be in the room lying right next to my brother and I'd feel like I was suffocating. I felt like I was about to die and I couldn't even move my body, I couldn't even reach over to touch my brother, I couldn't even speak to him to say help! At about the age of 17, I had reached a new level of being sold out to God. I simply made a new determined dedication to go deeper and to be more radically a servant of God. I considered myself a Jesus Freak! I had been preparing to go into ministry, I thought I might be a Pastor, Evangelist, or something like that. I was getting ready to go away to Bible College and around this age. I would walk up to winos and knock their beer bottles out of their hands and preach to them. I would interrupt drug buys and all kinds of stuff, preaching to repent and come to Jesus. This sounds crazy now but back then I believed no weapon formed against me shall prosper, I believed it was my duty to tell the World about Jesus and I was just brave, fearless, and foolish enough to do it. There was a spiritual mentor in my life at that time and he was one of the smartest men of God I've ever met. I remember being in his house and we were having a conversation about the Bible and at the end of our conversation he said to me, "Billy boy, I can see that you have grown, you have gone to another level in your dedication and your focus on God ". Then he says, "Not only do I see it but the Devil sees it also, so you need to be careful because he's coming for you! He sees that you are on this new higher level and his attacks are gonna be on a new level so get ready Billy boy." He wasn't lying! That same day my life changed and would never be the same again. Satan seemed closer than ever and would attack me harder than ever before. You won't believe some of the things that started happening to me that very same day.

Chapter Three

SATAN WAS
COMING FOR ME!

We left off in the last Chapter with the spiritual mentor in my life informing me that now that I had become more serious about God, that now the Devil was coming to get me more than ever. He said that I had become more serious and dedicated to God so I had gotten on the Devil's radar and he was coming for me to stop me. Shortly after that, maybe a couple of hours later, I walked into the house and my beloved dog, Otto, was acting strange. He had been my faithful buddy for many years, he was a very trained dog, He would sit when told, etc. He was a big gray German Shepherd with gray eyes. He was a beautiful, very kind, and sweet dog. He looked scary but he was very gentle &

very obedient. On this day, the same day of my warning, I walked into the house and Otto ran towards me, stopped in front of me, and just started barking at me, showing all his teeth and growling at me. I was shocked, I began looking around, thinking someone was behind me because I knew my best friend wasn't acting that way to me. I'm wondering what's going on. He never does this. He is responding to me like I was an intruder like he doesn't even recognize me. I realize that I am the only person in the house so he is doing this to me. He's looking right at me, walking slowly towards me, growling. Looking like he wanted to kill me. This is freaking me out, nothing I said to Otto calmed him down. I began preparing to defend myself then all of a sudden I remembered what my spiritual mentor said and I started talking in tongues and binding the Devil. When I started talking in tongues and praying, all of a sudden my dog calmed down and started wagging his tail. He lowered his head and walked up to me so I could rub him. That had never happened before, as a matter of fact, nothing even close had happened like that before or even since. So I was on high alert now, after the situation with my dog and after what the minister had said to me. Later that same day, my friends, Derick, Edgar, and I were all sitting down in the house, just talking and all of a sudden we heard a loud boom like somebody had kicked our back door in. The back door flung open and smacked loudly up against the wall. We were three boys from the hood in Detroit so immediately we grabbed anything close to us and prepared for battle. We assumed somebody was trying to break into the house and trying to rob us or something, so all three of us ran to the back door and we saw no one. The door was just wide open but it had been locked with two locks. To this day, I cannot explain it, none of us can. We thought maybe someone kicked the door in then ran after realizing we were home but It was wintertime, and snow was everywhere, so we looked out into the snow but we didn't see any footprints, none anywhere. This freaked us out so we simply closed the door and started praying, knowing something sinister and demonic was happening. We all were church boys so we immediately began praying and binding the Devil, etc. Then while we were praying the lamp on a table flew off the table and hit the floor like somebody smacked it and knocked it on the floor. Now all three of us were there and again that's the same day my dog acted up and I received my warning that the Devil was coming for me. Both of my boys Derick and Edgar are still alive and kicking and can bear witness to this story. There was another day, I don't remember how long it was after this but I know it was within the next few months. Derick and I kept noticing Edgar, our other roommate doing weird things. We would see him go into the basement and then a minute later we would see him come out of a bedroom. Derick and I looked at each other puzzled. We were like wait a minute, we never saw him come up here from the basement. Plus Edgar was acting odd, for instance, we would call him and he wouldn't respond, he would simply ignore us. We assumed he was mad about something. It was as if there were two different Edgars in the house. The Edgar walking past us and going to the basement was mean-faced and ignored us but the Edgar that came in and out of the bedroom was the normal friendly Edgar. One Edgar would speak to us and the other would just go past us and we wouldn't see him return, we would just see him go and then he would come from a different place. This happened about 3 times. We thought he was playing a joke on us, maybe he found a way to get from the basement to his bedroom. After confronting Edgar, I could tell he was genuinely confused by our questions, he thought we were playing a joke on him. I know this doesn't make any sense. It was strange like I said, he went to the basement, we didn't see him come back up, then the next thing I know he's coming out of a room acting totally different. Spooky, spooky stuff.

Chapter Four

SUCCUBUS

Sometime later it was now summertime. I was lying on the floor in the living room. Derek was lying on the couch in front of me and behind me was Edgar on another couch. So it was two couches in the living room and I was on the floor in between them. I had the fan on right in front of me as I slept on the floor. There were bedrooms but for whatever reason we were all asleep in the living room. We were probably up all night talking, cracking jokes, Bible studying, watching movies, or something like that. After we had all fallen asleep I was awakened by this absolutely beautiful woman standing over me. She was standing right above me as I lay down on the floor. As I look up at her, she smiles at me. I remember it so clearly like it happened last night. She had on a sexy red top & black stretch pants, she was barefoot and her hair was in a long ponytail. She was beautiful! After I look up and see her standing there, I immediately get up and start following her to the bedroom. While I'm following her, I'm taking off my clothes as I walk because I know without a doubt that I'm about to have sex with this girl. I am just following this beautiful woman and when we get to this intersection in front of the bathroom and between the two bedrooms, She Vanishes! I immediately started looking for her everywhere. I began turning on lights, and looking under beds and in closets. I could not find her so now I'm freaking out. Was I dreaming? I'm pinching myself, smacking my face to verify I'm awake. I'm still standing up in this hallway looking around like oh my God, what's going on! I go into the bathroom and look in the mirror wondering what the heck just happened. This girl was standing right here in front of me. I felt like I was losing my mind. To help you understand my dismay beyond the obvious, there were several internal problems with this for me at this time. The first issue was that I was saving myself for marriage and I wasn't having sex, so to be in the mindset where I'm following this woman to the bedroom, taking off my clothes getting ready to have sex with her. That was a humiliating spiritual blow to my Christianity. Secondly, I didn't ask who she was, I didn't ask her name, I didn't ask how did you get into my house. I just got up and started following her, taking off my clothes ready to have sex with this beautiful woman. Again to put this in perspective, I am a guy who has ex-girlfriends who crack jokes on me to this day because if we begin getting hot and heavy kissing and if at any point the kissing or petting gets too intense and I feel like we might be about to have sex, I would get up and run out of the house and down the street because I was fleeing fornication, literally! I was not trying to have sex until I was married and so for this situation to have happened, it shook me in so many different ways. After several minutes of washing my face, looking at myself in the mirror, and questioning everything that had occurred. I eventually go back to the living room, get back down on the floor, and move the fan. Then I lay in a completely different way because I want to make sure when I wake up tomorrow that I have evidence that this was not a dream. So I just rearranged everything. The next morning after I woke up everything was just as I had set it before going back to sleep. That was not a dream, my world was shaken. I was certain that a spirit had visited me that night. The fact that I could be so easily manipulated by this demon spirit upset me deeply. At this time I was very familiar with demons and spiritual warfare, even though this was the first time anything had ever happened to me like that. I hated how I felt like I was a victim to Satan, like I was helpless to resist this Succubus and again this was coming from a guy who was not having sex, who was saving himself for marriage and I was ready to just lose it all to this ghost, demon, spirit or whatever.

Chapter Five

CASTING OUT DEMONS

Sometime later my boy Derick had invited me to his old church, a church he left several years before and I went because we were in a Gospel Rap Group called "Theopneustos" which means, "God Breathed" in Hebrew. Since we were going to be performing at that church we were checking out the logistics of everything to be sure to give our best performance like we always did. Derrick had grown out of that church; he had left that church and moved on. So he was shocked when I fell in love with that church and I wanted to join it. It was a deliverance ministry and the pastor talked a lot about the Devil, demons spirits, and spiritual warfare since I was battling evil spirits all the time. I was intrigued. I felt like this church could help me defend myself better against the enemy. In that church, demons were a part of the ministry. They were almost welcome to attend service there because it was believed that demons interrupting service was evidence that we were doing something right because the Devil was trying to stop us. The pastor, testimony service, every deacon, prophet, evangelist and Sunday school teacher equipped us to defend ourselves and our loved ones against the onslaught of the Devil and his demons. We were learning the names of demons, different spirits, and how to do exorcisms or as we called it casting out demons. At this church people were regularly demon-possessed, witches were continually coming in and around the church placing spells on the ministry. We know this not only because we would find different things strategically placed outside around the church but because many times witches would come in the church harassing members, possessed with demons, talking in deep eerie voices, and too strong for several men to handle. I stayed at that church for many years becoming the youngest deacon in the church's history at the time and eventually becoming the youth pastor. I even met and married the mother of my children at that church. She can give you many stories of wrestling with Witches and Satan himself at that church. As a matter of fact, two days before writing this Chapter she was reminding me about all the witches and evil spirits that she dealt with at that church.   All kinds of crazy stuff was going on so I was excited and attracted to this church that my man Derick had grown past but I was all in. It was something new to me and it was exciting and I loved it. This deliverance ministry introduced me to all these books about spiritual warfare and demons and these books scared me and intrigued me at the same time I also felt like they empowered me because I felt that to defeat the enemy you gotta know his tricks or his tactics and so these books were arming me and preparing me for battle.   I was learning about the names of different demons and how to cast them out. I learned how to talk to the demon to find out his goals and his purposes and all of that kind of stuff I was learning about territorial demons, spirits over neighborhoods, demon principalities over cities, evil ruling powers over our country, spirits that ruled over buildings and stuff like that. I learned how to spot demons, in the room or inside of people. I was getting a whole bunch of demon education and I felt like a soldier in the army of the Lord equipping myself to do battle with the enemy. I was there for several years and saw so much unbelievable stuff. I'm just going to talk about a few things I saw at this church. I wanna stick with things that can be verified by other witnesses. There was a man who got up out of his seat in church and started walking on the back of the pews towards the front of the church. Now look, if you know about how most pews are, there's a seat and there's this little thin back of it that you lean your back on. This man walked across the tops of the pews up to the front where the pastor was preaching to attack the pastor. I believe I have pretty good balance but I cannot imagine walking across the back of those pews plus it wasn't like he was looking down at his feet he was looking directly at the pastor with a very hateful look on his face. The Deacons and I grabbed this brother and held him down, all the sudden he began to go crazy and started talking in other languages, cursing in different voice tones and he reminded me of the little girl from Exodus only he didn't spin his head around, he didn't spit the green vomit but a lot of the other stuff was similar and that happened a lot at that church. I remember a young girl coming into the church, she came in and was chanting all this witchcraft stuff and trying to curse the church and all of us, so a bunch of people grabbed her and tried to pray for her and cast the demon out and she started cussing people out, doing stuff like the girl in the Exorcist, saying things and sounding crazy with deep voices and stuff like that. It took me and several grown big muscle-bound men to try to hold this little girl down. She was so strong that I was sore after trying to hold her down and it was crazy. Just by the looks of her, It would seem that I should be able to hold her by myself with little issue but several of us could barely hold her down and we were all just yelling at the demons inside her, binding and loosing, casting out demons because she had many. We know this because we asked the demon how many were inside this girl and they told us "Legion". I know right, straight out of the movies or the Bible. The pastor was putting Anointed Oil all over her. We are all talking in tongues, yelling out Scriptures, yelling "Come Out" to the demons, asking each demon's name and purpose. There was no order. We were all speaking on top of each other and at the same time feeling that by all of us attacking these spirits together they surely had no chance of surviving. The pastor was pleading the blood over the congregation and warning them to stay praying in the Spirit because when the evil spirits leave this girl they will try to enter into you if you are not in the spirit. I think this lasted for two hours or something. That was crazy but this kind of thing happened often. We were trying to set these people free, we felt like they were being tormented by demons and it was our job to free them. There would be people naked on all fours, eating the carpet in the church, I could go on and on, with this kind of crazy stuff. I began to look down at all my previous churches before this one because they obviously in my mind weren't doing the work of the Lord because the Devil wasn't attacking their church services like he was ours so obviously they were no threat to the Devil. Our saying was that if the Devil isn't attacking you it's because you're no threat to his kingdom and if you were no threat you were basically working for the Devil.

Chapter Six

THE WITCH BOOK

One day some people at church were excited about a book they were reading which was the true story of this Witch who had gotten saved and had given her life to God. In this book, the lady gives her story about how she had been a very powerful witch, according to her she was a leader in the Witch community with a high stature because of her powers. She explained how she would put spells on and torment many people. She said she could astral project out of her body and go to a person's home and punish them physically. This ex-Witch said she used to send demons to torment people, among other things she would talk about in this book that she used to do to people. Then something happened to her and she found God or God found her, however you want to say it. She gave her life to God and became a Christian and because she turned her back on her witchcraft community they had in turn put a spiritual bounty on her head or a hit out on her for her betrayal. Especially since she was such a high-ranking, powerful, and respected witch. I can't remember the name of this book and neither can my old acquaintances from that church although most seem to remember the book just not the title. In the book, this lady details how a lot of horrible things began happening to her. Witches who used to serve under her as well as Witches and Warlocks who were her contemporaries on the same level, would come against her and attack her. They would send demons to her to torment her every night and other witches would astral project themselves to her home to punish her. She said as she lay in bed trying to sleep they would come and attack her physically and it's what happened to her every night for years and she would be in spiritual warfare battling and fighting these witches and demons every night. As you read her story, she would eventually win those battles but it would be after much pain and suffering, every night. She said she could barely sleep and was always in pain the next day. This was crazy to me and this went on for years but the fact that she had to fight, battle, and suffer like that for her life against demons and witches every night for years bothered me immensely! That coupled with all the years of my battles with demons and the Devil as well as my own experience in church exorcisms that lasted for hours, where it seemed like we squeaked out victories against the demons possessing those people. My own experiences coupled with what I read about this lady in that book wounded me terribly. I was in great mental distress, confusion, and anger. I remember being extremely pissed at God! Yes, I admit it, I was upset with God, I felt betrayed on behalf of this Ex-witch and myself. I went to God in prayer with tears in my eyes, crying mad, yelling, "Why would you save this woman and let her suffer like that for years God?" "She was better off being a witch". "Why would I go and tell anybody about coming to You and giving their life to You God, if then you gonna let them struggle and suffer through painful attacks, every night for years and years?" Then I remember the focus shifting to me talking about myself to God. I'm serving you faithfully, I pray and read the Bible daily, I tell people about you and your Son Jesus, I never miss a church service, I pay my tithes faithfully and fast often! I can't understand why all this craziness keeps happening, why would you allow this to happen to me for years? I then threatened God. I know that sounds crazy but I feel like I lost my mind, feeling betrayed by God. I believe those feelings had been hidden in my heart for years but I was simply too afraid to express them. But in that moment the floodgates were opened, allowing honesty to escape my religious walls, mingled with a lot of tears, hopelessness, and rage. I threatened God yelling, "I will never attempt to Preach the Gospel, Win Souls to Christ, or Minister to anyone else ever again if You don't give me some answers God. That witch lived a better and more peaceful life being a witch than she did becoming a Christian". "How could You allow the Devil to abuse Your Children like that? Why had he been allowing that?" I doubled down and vowed in my anger, "I will never tell anyone else about you because they are better off without you, they need some protection, you betta tell me something or I'm done!" When I was done letting out all my frustrations, tears, anger, and upset feelings, I calmed down and finally became silent. I still felt betrayed and powerless but I was now finally calm. I felt like God said something to me. I believe I heard God say something to me that would change my entire life. It wasn't very deep or complicated, in fact, it seemed too simple.

I believe I heard God say "The only reason that Woman in your book had those horrible things happening to her is because she believed they could happen to her". I froze in my tracks at what I heard then I believe He said, "She had faith in the other witches as well as those demons' abilities to attack her and to harm her."

Sad to admit that I had too much religious programming and too many personal experiences of demonic or spiritual attacks to buy into what I heard. So although that statement rang true in my spirit and kinda seemed like a little common sense, it didn't take root in me just yet. But it was a seed that was planted in me and it began to grow, slowly.

Chapter Seven

JESUS - VS - SATAN

I realize now that I subconsciously had put Jesus and the Devil on equal footing, as though they were simply equal adversaries or one side of the coin. Yin and Yang. One was good and one was bad but they were equal in power and ability and I had given God a slight edge in power over both. This was all subconscious and emotional. Honestly, I would have never admitted to this publicly or even to myself, out of fear of God or just simple denial. Mentally and in my heart, I felt like the equal status I gave Satan and Jesus came from years of spiritual battles, struggles, and the way the Devil could affect my life as compared to how God could. It seemed like the Devil had more physical ability to do stuff almost like he was more powerful in everyday circumstances, while Jesus was relegated to more spiritual power to help my life. Maybe because I felt like the Devil was closer and God was farther and because of the Devil's vicinity he was more powerful whereas God was far away in Heaven. I don't know, but subconsciously I just viewed them as kind of equal, with God having a little more power and I've learned from disgusting this idea over the years, that a lot of Christians have that same subconscious feeling they just don't admit it just like I would never have admitted to that either. After I became secure and bold enough to admit those feelings it seemed as though other people would feel a little more free to say yeah I feel that way about God and Satan too. Those feelings are understandable, especially when it seems like the Devil is actively attacking your mind, your body, your children, your family, your church, your job, your finances, etc. and it seems that you have to beg and petition God to help you or your family. Almost as if God is busy with the world but the Devil and his demons are focused on you. I want to clearly state that I no longer feel this way and I'm hoping that this book will free your mind from these conscious and subconscious beliefs as well.

Chapter Eight

TRICKS OF THE ENEMY

Gradually, over time, I began to start seeing the Devil differently. He started to become less and less powerful to me, less strong in my eyes. I begin speaking to demons and casting out demons with just a few words as opposed to taking hours of yelling and struggling. I began to slowly start seeing God and Jesus as much more powerful than the Devil. But I was still being attacked mentally and physically. After I was married, I would be attacked in the bed, lying right next to my wife. Many times I tried to reach out and touch or use my voice to get my wife's attention so that she could help me but I never was successful. Unfairly, I subconsciously held a grudge against her for this because she claimed to always be in tune with the devil's movements, she stayed in spiritual warfare against the Devil and seemed to always know when he was up to something but she could never tell when I was being attacked lying right next to her. But she didn't deserve that. As I write this, I can recall the fear of death as I felt this invisible presence sitting on my chest and placing what seemed like a claw or hand right under my nose so that I could barely breathe. So I would try to shake myself free, I would try mumbling under my breath, rebuking the Devil, speaking in tongues in my head, asking God for help, and anything I could think of all in my head or under my breath until the demon would get off of me and leave. As time passed, Satan and his demons were still slowly decreasing in power in my mind. Eventually, in 2001 I wrote a play about the Devil called, "Tricks on the Enemy" in an attempt to expose the tricks of the enemy. In the play, one of the main characters was the Devil, but every time I would audition somebody to play the Devil, they were talking in some deep, exaggerated voice being overly dramatic and I kept saying, "No, no, no. If the Devil talked like that to us for real, we would know it's him." "He would never be able to trick us that way. "He talks just like you talk, so please talk normally". No matter how much I tried to explain it to people auditioning for that role, they never would get it and so out of frustration. I ended up just doing it myself. It was one of the best things I could have ever done in my life. It was a blessing, I felt like. Maybe God set me up where nobody could get that part, where no one could understand what I was looking for on purpose, so I could play it. In the script and on stage, I made the Devil very weak and foolish. His only real power in the play was to be sneaky, manipulative, and deceptive. His talent was the ability to trick you into doing something to hurt yourself. But outside of that, he was no match for God or his angels. I had a regular angel named Tyrone in the play that constantly punked the Devil throughout the play culminating in an awesome fight scene with choreographed, flips, martial arts, stick fighting, and even slow motion action all while the hit song, "Kung Fu Fighting" by Carl Douglas played, to the audiences' delight. The more I did the play, the weaker and more foolish I portrayed the Devil. As years passed, while doing this. I began to believe even more that what I was portraying was how the Devil really was. He was becoming stupid, foolish, nothing, not even a real threat. I know now that new Neural Pathways were being developed in my brain. This new view of Satan and his demons began to become more real to me. The Devil and his demons were becoming weak and insignificant in my mind and my heart, to the point where I looked up and months had passed since I had been hit by the devil or since any demon had landed on my chest and put pressure on me. My breathing was no longer being hindered. Honestly, normally this is something that happened a couple of times per week and at this point, months passed and nothing was happening. Eventually, I forgot about it and it just went away. It was as if the less I thought of the Devil, the less he could do, which again coincides with what I believe God told me about the Witch who had come to Christ. They could only do those horrible things to me because I believed they could. In my life today, demon-possessed people never appear in my presence anymore. I stopped spending all my prayer time in Spiritual Warfare, fighting and battling demons. Instead, I began to have conversations with God and simply began talking to him in an attempt to get to know Him better. Long story short, it has been well over a decade since a demon has hit me, spoke to me, frightened me, choked me, held me down, or anything of the sort. I haven't had to rebuke, bind, or battle with the Devil or his demons for over 10 years now. I'm no longer afraid of the dark. I no longer see flashes of some spirit or person go past my face. I never feel eerily cold in supposedly spooky or haunted places. I no longer have frightening feelings in a dark room or like something is sneaking up on me. I'm never worried that if I'm watching some TV show with somebody quoting some kind of witch chants, evil spirits are going to come up in my apartment, etc, with no concern or fear whatsoever. In recent years, I've talked to witches and even a Satan worshiper and it had no negative effects on me, not one bit. I can sit there and talk to them about the love of God or just be their friend. Without any fear of demonic attack, demonic spirits jumping on me and following me and taking me over, and all the other fear-based things about demons I used to believe. I don't even own any anointing oil right now, my walls are clean and fresh, with no oil stains, LOL. I am Free, plus I feel Free and You can Be and Feel Free too.

Chapter Nine

THE FALLEN ANGEL

I have heard all of my life that Satan is a fallen angel and I'm sure that you have likely heard the same but what If I told you that was a myth? Would you believe me If I told you that there are no Scriptures in the Bible, no verses, no passages, from the Old Testament to the New, there is not even one that says that Satan is a fallen angel. I used to do myths of the Bible on my Facebook page and The Fallen Angel Myth was the first one I ever did. I used to put them up regularly maybe once or twice a week and I did it for ego purposes. I put them up there as a way of showing off what I knew. I knew it was going to drive people crazy. They were going to try to prove me wrong but trust me if I placed it on a public forum like that I already won the argument before I started. I had already studied and I knew what I was talking about. I slept like a baby knowing my religious friends were up all night searching the Scriptures to prove me wrong, to no avail. Likely, you may even be itching to put this book down and go scouring the Bible right now to prove me wrong. The reason I stopped doing those Bible myths was because as I began maturing, I wanted to get away from stroking my ego and doing things for ego purposes and the only reason that I'm bringing this myth back up is because of the lesson it taught me about my faith. I learned that so many things I previously believed were in the Bible, were only assumed through the veil of Sermons from the pulpit, man's opinions, misunderstandings, or prejudices. A lot of things I was taught from the pulpit, I had taken them as fact. They were perfect in sermons to get points or agendas across but they were not true in the context of scripture. This book shines the light on many of those bible myths but this myth is the easiest example and most fun in my opinion. Especially because of my personal lesson with this myth. Back in 1988, there was a Minister named Jerry Tempton, a very wise man. I was a teenager, who studied the Bible every day but I was not on his level. I was in a Gospel rap group and Jerry was the Manager. We had a song about the Devil called StarChild and while discussing the rap song, I mentioned something about Lucifer, The Fallen Anger, and Jerry said The Devil is not a Fallen angel he was never an angel. I thought he was joking so I laughed and said yes he is, that's in the Bible. Jerry laughed out loud, then calmly looked at me and said, "Show me". When he hit me with this, in my heart and mind, I knew he was wrong and I was gonna get him. I was excited about finally being able to correct a man who I consider one of the most intelligent men I've ever met. I could not wait to prove him wrong. I didn't say anything else, I just said, "Okay, I'm gonna look into it". I was excited! I'm finally gonna teach Jerry something about the Bible. I was 100 percent certain that the Scriptures say that Satan is a fallen angel. I was certain that I had not only heard it stated by all the biggest Preachers on the planet but that I had personally read it in the Bible myself. Jerry was going down! All that day and all night until I fell asleep from exhaustion, I studied and searched the Bible to prove him wrong. I woke up the next morning still baffled because I couldn't find it. I called people I believed learned in Bible knowledge, even a few Bible college graduates. They agreed with me that it was in the bible but none of us could find it. I continued searching all day until I was supposed to meet with Jerry later that evening. Embarrassed and frustrated, I humbly went to him and said, "You were right". He said, "I know Billy boy, I was never in doubt". LOL. Honestly, this revelation shook my world. I learned something that day about my unflinching belief in knowledge about Biblical beliefs that are not supported by the Bible. It shook up my world and planted a seed in me that made me realize that there were likely more things I believed about the Bible, and some things I believed about the Devil that had absolutely no biblical facts and zero biblical influence, yet I believed it with every fiber of my being. It was an embarrassing and enlightening lesson and I'm sharing it with you now. I began to question things the preachers said in the pulpit. I've personally heard sermons and read books by very famous ministers that I loved, adored, and was convinced knew the Bible but they all called Satan a fallen angel and I did too. Like I said, I swore that I had even read it in the Bible myself but it was not there. Maybe Satan is a fallen angel but To conclude that scripture states Satan was ever an angel, that he fell from heaven in a heavenly war, that he convinced a third of the angels to fight with him, and that he is currently a fallen angel we have to create a jigsaw puzzle from many different verses of scripture to form an image of a being that fits our imagination or our taught beliefs. But if those puzzle pieces are read correctly, in the context of scripture as they were originated, they do not form that picture.

I realized that I had a filter placed over me that blinded me and blurred how I saw the Bible, the Scriptures, and the Devil. With this revelation, I had a paradigm shift in my thinking and now I want to plant a seed in you. Maybe there are things we think we know about the Scriptures that we don't really know and maybe this revelation will wake us up to be more open to see that there may be some truths that we might not see accurately, there may be some misconceptions we have about the Bible, about God, about the Devil, about ourselves and our Christianity. If we can see things in context as opposed to through the filters and blinders that have been put over our eyes to hinder us or control how we view things then we are more likely to be free from confusion and biblical misinterpretation. Allow me to clarify this revelation for You. First, the Bible never calls Satan, Lucifer, the Devil, or Beelzebub an angel even before he was supposedly being kicked from Heaven. (We will get more into that war in Heaven in the Chapter on Lucifer). The Bible does call Lucifer a Cherubim but the Bible never confuses angels with Cherubim only Preachers do that. Even the biblical account of how Cherubim look is extremely different from how angels appear in Scripture. According to Scripture, Cherubim have wings, have four faces: that of a man, a lion, an ox, and an eagle.

Even more, detail was given about Lucifer In Ezekiel's Chapter Twenty-Eight. It is said, that "every precious stone was thy covering, the sardius, topaz, and the diamond, the beryl, the onyx, and the jasper, the sapphire, the emerald, and the carbuncle, and gold: the workmanship of thy tabrets and thy pipes was prepared in thee in the day that thou wast created". Compare that to almost every sighting of an angel in Scripture recorded as looking like a man. There are several times documented in Scripture where angels were mistaken for mere men. This happens so much in Scripture that many Bible scholars believe it is possible that angels were men who behaved Heavenly or the word angel could be an Ancient term for Men of God or Ministers. Lastly, the closest verse of Scripture that even alludes to the idea of Satan being an angel is the metaphoric representation of him having the ability to appear as an angel of Light. Which can be interpreted in context as having the ability to appear as a minister of light or minister of good but only in appearance in order to deceive. If you were already aware of this myth, please accept this confirmation but if this is a new revelation for you then I hope this simple truth that Satan isn't according to scripture a fallen angel, allows you to let down your guard a little so that you can remain open-minded to the intriguing and controversial things in this book.

Chapter Ten

THE DEVIL & THE SATAN

There is a lot of misunderstanding surrounding these words, Satan or Devil. Over time it has morphed into the name of the Evil One, even though it was never intended to be used that way. Satan simply means adversary or opposer. Consider this biblical fact that some very good people were called a Satan in scripture. David, for instance, was described as a Satan (adversary). In his attempt to flee from King Saul, David decided to go to the land of the Philistines, where Saul would certainly not follow him. David lived there for a year and 4 months (1 Samuel 27:7) under the employment of Achish, the Philistine king of Gath. But many of the Philistines feared and distrusted David: He was an Adversary to them and they considered him a Satan to them. The word adversary is used many times throughout the Old Testament. It is literally HaSatan, Ha meaning the and Satan meaning to act as an adversary. It is mostly used as a verb denoting action taken, not as a person. The word Satan is a title, it can be referring to an action but it is not a name. Strangely though, almost all English translations drop the "Ha" (The), turning this Hebrew title into a name: Satan. The first time the word "Satan" is used in the Hebrew Bible in reference to a supernatural figure comes from Numbers 22:22, which describes the angel of Yahweh confronting Balaam on his donkey: "Balaam's departure aroused the wrath of Elohim, and the angel of Yahweh stood in the road as a Satan against him. Please pay attention to this one, "the angel of the Lord" is described as "a satan," who opposes the infamous Balaam. So even the angelic messenger who represents the will and authority of God himself can take on the function of a satan. The Hebrew term Satan is a generic noun meaning accuser or adversary and is derived from a verb meaning primarily, to obstruct, or oppose. In the Septuagint, the Hebrew ha-Satan is used but in the books of

Zechariah and Job it is translated by the Greek word diabolos (slanderer), the same word in the Greek New Testament from which the English word "Devil" is derived. Nearly every Old Testament passage in which satan appears is in reference to a human who stands somehow in an oppositional relationship to another human, there are only about 4 instances in the entire Old Testament where it can be argued that the satan may be talking of a supernatural being. The Devil: This was borrowed from the Greek word diabolos, "slanderer", from diaballein, "to slander", "across, through" and ballein, "to hurl", probably akin to the Sanskrit gurate, "he lifts up". The use of daimon in the New Testament's original Greek text caused the Greek word to be applied to the Judeo-Christian concept of an evil spirit by the early second century AD. But it was originally used to label a person who slanders or hurls accusations. Same as Satan. Devil is used more in the New Testament and Satan more in the old. Jesus rebuked Peter by saying, "Get thee behind me, Satan!" Is it possible that we are so used to blaming everybody else for our actions that we immediately jumped to the conclusion that the Devil must have crawled up into one of Jesus Christ's disciples and was speaking through him? But Scripture doesn't even hint that something like that happened. Peter was simply being an adversary to what Jesus was trying to do, and Jesus simply called him out for what he was doing. He said get thee behind me adversary. Now I'm not saying that a literal Satan doesn't exist. Just pointing out the fact that this comment from Jesus in context does absolutely nothing to prove a literal Satan does exist. I think it's more likely to prove he doesn't exist. In Judaism, the word Satan is used as a verb. It does not refer to a person, rather it refers to temptations or difficulties to overcome.

Chapter Eleven

LUCIFER

Currently in churches and pulpits all over the world, Lucifer is another name for Satan. But was that how the original readers believed or understood? Is it possible that the early church had a much different understanding of who Lucifer was? In 1667 John Milton famously used Lucifer as the name for Satan in his poem Paradise Lost. But no verse in the Bible says, "Lucifer is Satan." In fact, there is some dispute as to whether Lucifer is even a proper name in the Bible. Lucifer originates from, Helel, or the shining one. Helel was translated into Latin as Lucifer. In Roman mythology, Lucifer meaning light-bringer was the classical name for the planet Venus or "(the early one that shines in the morning.) There is no star (kokav) in the Isaiah passage (although an awful lot of translations use star). Lucifer as a name does not show up in the Bible anywhere. "The Shining One" is a title, just like Ha-Satan is a title ("The Adversary").

A character referred to as "Lucifer" appears in Isaiah 14, as an insulting rant against the king of Babylon. (Isaiah 14:4). The wicked king, who oppressed other nations, is brought to ruin. God has broken the king of Babylon's scepter (Isaiah 14:5) and laid him low (verse 8). The defeated king of Babylon is pictured as entering the place of the dead, where other departed kings are waiting for him with excitement.

"" You also have become weak, as we are; you have become like us." All your pomp has been brought down to the grave, along with the noise of your harps; maggots are spread out beneath you and worms cover you" (Isaiah 14:10–11). The prophecy against the king of Babylon continues with these popular verses that are preached from pulpits often in reference to the devil but in context are speaking to a literal person, the despised King of Babylon: "How you are fallen from Heaven, O Lucifer, son of the morning!

How you are cut down to the ground, You who weakened the nations! For you have said in your heart: 'I will ascend into Heaven, I will exalt my throne above the stars of God; I will also sit on the mount of the congregation. On the farthest sides of the north;

I will ascend above the heights of the clouds, I will be like the Most High.' Yet you shall be brought down to Sheol, To the lowest depths of the Pit" (Isaiah 14:12–15, NKJV).

The King James Version and the New King James Version have "Lucifer" in Isaiah 14:12, but other translations have "morning star" (NIV), "Day Star" (ESV), or "shining one" (NET). Is the term meant as a proper name, or simply as a metaphor for the king's greatness? If you read ancient texts from all over the world they are overflowing with God-like and supernatural dialog in reference to Kings from every nation, throughout history. In context and without assumptions, these scriptures clearly show that the primary interpretation of

Isaiah 14 is that of a prophecy against the human king of Babylon. However, the poetic descriptions of his grandeur, his sin, and his fate are so extravagant as to cause many scholars to consider a secondary interpretation like a reference to Satan. Lucifer is Latin for light-bearer and was the name given to the morning star, or the planet Venus. These passages, originally written in ancient Hebrew, on face value, refer to the tyrannical Babylonian king who boasts of his conquests but who is "about to be cast to the ground." Using logic and ignoring the hyperbolic writing that is used all over the bible, especially in the Old Testament reading that Lucifer is said to have fallen from Heaven, can't refer to a human being, a human wouldn't survive that kind of fall, so it must refer to a supernatural being like Satan. UCLA Professor Henry Ansgar Kelly confirms the idea that people likely assumed Lucifer was a supernatural being because of the fall from heaven reading. The Professor states, "Some later church leaders found this reasoning persuasive, and so did many who followed them, leading to this widespread belief. The only mentions of Lucifer in the New Testament refer to Jesus." "Jesus is called 'Lucifer' or 'the morning star' because he represents a new beginning." Similarly, a passage in the Gospel of Luke, when Jesus reports having seen "Satan fall like lightning," has been misinterpreted, according to Kelly. "Jesus saw the fall in the past because he had the vision the day before he described it to the apostles," Kelly said. "But Jesus is referring to a future fall [of Satan] from his position as God's attorney general."

Chapter Twelve

BEELZEBUB

The Old Testament uses the name Beelzebub to speak of the God of Ekron. We do not see it being used as a possible name for Satan until the writings of the New Testament. From Latin, Beelzebub, prince of Devils, from Greek Beelzeboub, from Hebrew Baʿal zĕbhūbh, a Philistine God, literally, lord of flies. The biblical source for the name Beelzebub is in the Books of Kings (2 Kings 1:2–3, 6, 16), written Ba'al-zəbûb, referring to a deity worshiped by the Philistines in the city of Ekron. The title Baal, meaning "Lord" in Ugaritic, was used in conjunction with a descriptive name of a specific God. In 2 Kings 1:2, we read about the Israel King Ahaziah falling through a window in his upstairs room in Samaria. He sends messengers to get information about an entity called

Beelzebub. Beelzebub was also known as the God of Ekron. Ekron was a city inhabited by the Philistines and one of the capitals of the Philistine Pentapolis. Ekron was torn down by many rival people groups but was destroyed by the Babylonians in 603 B.C. under the leadership of King Nebuchadnezzar. Beelzebub means "lord of the flies." In Hebrew and Jewish literature, the name is translated to mean "lord of dung" or "lord of filth." Images of Beelzebub portray him as a fly or flying insect. Scholars have learned that the image of the fly as Beelzebub derives from either the thought that he is a sun God that brings the flies or he is the God invoked to drive flies away from the sacrifice. Beelzebub is the Greek form of the word Baal-zebub. There are connections to Baal worship in conjunction with the worship of Beelzebub. Baal was a Canaanite fertility God in the Old Testament. The term zebub means "exalted dwelling." When we put those two terms together, we have the name Prince of Demons.

Beelzebub as a reference to Satan is linked to the Pharisees. The name became a bitter, scornful word and Jews began to use it as a reference to Satan. In Matthew 12:22-28 it reads: "Then a demon-oppressed man who was blind and mute was brought to him, and he healed him so that the man spoke and saw. And all the people were amazed, and said, "Can this be the Son of David?" But when the Pharisees heard it, they said, "It is only by Beelzebul, the prince of demons, that this man casts out demons." Knowing their thoughts, he said to them, "Every kingdom divided against itself is laid waste, and no city or house divided against itself will stand. And if Satan casts out Satan, he is divided against himself. How then will his kingdom stand? And if I cast out demons by Beelzebul, by whom do your sons cast them out? Therefore they will be your judges. But if it is by the Spirit of God that I cast out demons, then the kingdom of God has come upon you." In the above verses the Pharisees are accusing Jesus of casting out demons by the power of "Beelzebub, the prince of demons." Matthew 12:24 states; "when the Pharisees heard it, they said, "It is only by Beelzebul, the prince of demons, that this man casts out demons." In Judaism, the word Satan is used as a verb. It does not refer to a person, rather it refers to temptation or difficulty to overcome. The Old Testament uses the name Beelzebub to speak of the God of Ekron. We do not see it being used as a name for Satan until the writings of the New Testament. As previously mentioned, we only find the name Beelzebub referenced once in the Old Testament by King Ahaziah when he is injured from a fall. This reference is found in 2 Kings 1:1- 16. There is no description of Beelzebub given in the text, most likely because this deity was well-known in the land. Beelzebub is referenced only in the Gospels of the New Testament. In the book of Matthew, we find the Pharisees using this term to describe Jesus. They were mocking him for the miracles he had done. Jesus also uses this term in Chapter 10 to teach the disciples as he sends them out to the mission field. Again, in the book of Mark, the Pharisees use this term to describe how Jesus was driving out demons.

Luke Chapter 11 is another instance where we see this term used.

In ancient religions, Beelzebub was associated with sacrifices. He was invoked to drive away the flies that always came as sacrifices were made and blood was shed. During the time of Jesus, Beelzebub became a prince of demons. The name becomes a reference to Satan and a distinct insult to Jesus. Beelzebub was believed to be someone who could perform exorcisms.

Chapter Thirteen

WAR IN HEAVEN

Before the creation of Man, Satan rebelled against God and a Great War broke out in Heaven. Satan convinced a third of the Angels to fight with him. Satan lost that battle and was banished to the earth where he is no longer a Heavenly Angel but the Prince of Darkness and the third of Heaven's Angels that followed Satan are now Demons on earth tormenting mankind in service of Satan. Reads like a sci-fi movie script, but it is in scripture. In Revelation 12:7–10 (NIV) it reads, "Then war broke out in heaven. Michael and his angels fought against the dragon, and the dragon and his angels fought back. 8 But he was not strong enough, and they lost their place in heaven. 9 The great dragon was hurled down—that ancient serpent called the devil, or Satan, who leads the whole world astray. He was hurled to the earth, and his angels with him."

This is an excellent example of how Christian teachings can become Bible doctrine. There is not a single verse in the entire Bible that tells us that the Devil sinned before the episode of Genesis Chapter 3, or that a third of the angels also fell either before humanity's fall or at the time of that fall. Rev 12:1–9 is the only passage that mentions a "third " of the angels (presumably because it says stars, not angels) and Satan or the serpent together. This passage is clear that the timing of this conflict involving a third of the assumed angels occurred at the same time as the first coming of the Messiah. The reference to the child born to rule the nations as being "caught up to God and his throne" is an explicit reference to the resurrection and ascension of Christ the Messiah—the key events that result in the defeat of Satan and the introduction of the kingdom of God on earth. We have to use our imaginations to twist these Scriptures to describe a Heavenly rebellion or war before the creation of humanity in Eden. Since there is no other passage in the Bible that uses the "third" language in conjunction with a Satanic conflict, the idea that Satan and one-third of the angels rebelled at that time is a traditional myth.

Chapter Fourteen

JOB'S ADVERSARY

The well-known conversation between God and the Devil is found in the Book of Job. Allow me to mention that many bible scholars believe the Book of Job is largely poetry. The speeches of Job, his three friends, and the Lord are all in poetic language. These speeches are 'framed' by a Prologue and Epilogue in narrative prose. The Hebrew term, "the satan" describes an adversarial role. It is not the name of a particular character. Some bible scholars consider Job a parable and not a true account of someone's life. Regardless, it is filled with symbolic language just as much of the Old Testament is and should not be taken literally. Angels can easily be interpreted as messengers or ministers of God. Sons of God can be interpreted as followers of God or servants of God. The adversary can be interpreted as the accuser, the satan, or the devil. None are names but only titles of actions. Most importantly it is written in the form of ancient songs or more accurately ancient poems. This book opens with an interesting scene. A heavenly meeting or gathering of sorts, where angels or people present themselves before God. The Adversary was among them. In Job, there is a conversation between God and the Adversary. God said to the Adversary, Job loves me, and no matter what you throw at him, he will never turn his back on me.

But the Adversary doesn't believe this human could have faith in, and love for, his God in times of trial. If Job was to lose all of his possessions, would he still cling to God? So the Adversary tested Job, and even after all that the Adversary did to Job, Job remained steadfast in his commitment to God. There's so much to this story, but there is one thing, in particular, to note: in this conversation between God and the Adversary, we read God's name Yahweh, but we never see the name of the

Adversary. Could that be because the adversary is a title or an action? Could the adversary simply be a representation of an unnamed person who took on the job of the adversary at that moment? Maybe or maybe not but we are very clearly told God's name in those passages.

Chapter Fifteen

SATAN IS REAL?

A llow me to confirm that my goal is not to insist that the Devil doesn't exist but only to prove that many church-taught ideas of scripture concerning Satan are misunderstood and misinterpreted. Verses about Satan or the Devil in context, mostly referred to a human antagonist as opposed to a supernatural being of evil. If Satan is a real supernatural, evil being. According to scripture, he is not the enemy of God, his name isn't Lucifer and he isn't even evil. And as far as leading Adam and Eve astray, could that simply be a bad rap stemming from a case of mistaken identity?

UCLA Professor Henry Ansgar Kelly says, "There's little or no evidence in the Bible for most of the characteristics and deeds commonly attributed to Satan," insists Kelly with four decades in what he describes as "the Devil business." In "Satan: A Biography" (Cambridge Press), Henry Ansgar Kelly puts forth the most comprehensive case ever made for sympathy for the Devil, arguing that the Bible actually provides a kinder, gentler version of the infamous antagonist than typically thought. "A strict reading of the Bible shows Satan to be less like Darth Vader and more and more like an overzealous prosecutor," said Kelly, a UCLA professor emeritus of English and the former director of the university's Center for Medieval and Renaissance Studies. Kelly started his academic career at a Jesuit seminary and was ordained in four of the seven holy orders on the way to the priesthood, including the order of exorcist. Kelly says, "Satan's not so much the proud and angry figure who turns away from God as [he is] a Joseph McCarthy or J. Edgar Hoover. Satan's basic intention is to uncover wrongdoing and treachery, however overzealous and unscrupulous the means. But he's still part of God's administration." The view runs in opposition to the beliefs held by many

Christians and others about key religious concepts like original sin and the nature of good and evil. "If Satan isn't really in opposition to God and he isn't really evil, then that means the fight between good and evil isn't an authentic part of Christianity," Kelly said. "What I'm saying will be scandalous to some people." "It was at that time that I started my campaign to rehabilitate the Devil — to deliver him from evil, as it were," Kelly said. "Satan: A Biography" is the culmination of more than 40 years of research into the Devil and the religious and cultural traditions that have grown up around him. The book is Kelly's third on the topic. When it comes to the Old Testament, Kelly insists that Satan's profile is considerably lower than commonly thought and significantly less menacing. By Kelly's count, Satan only appears three times in the 45 books that make up the pre-Christian Scriptures, the best known being in the Book of Job. On each occasion, Satan is still firmly part of what Kelly calls "God's administration," and his activities are done at the behest of "the Big Guy." But his actions aren't evil so much as consistent with the translation of "Devil" and "Satan," which literally means "adversary" in Greek and Hebrew, respectively. "His job is to test people's virtue and to report their failures," Kelly said. This is not to say, however, that Kelly contends that Satan is likable. "Jesus doesn't like him, and Paul doesn't like him," Kelly explained. "He represents the old guard in the Heavenly bureaucracy, and everyone longs for him to be disbarred as the chief accuser of humankind." Meanwhile, in passages in Luke, Matthew, Corinthians, and elsewhere in the New Testament, Satan continues to act as a tester, enforcer, and prosecutor but not as God's enemy, Kelly points out. "Everyone else has said that by the time Satan gets to the New Testament, he is evil, he's an enemy of God, but that's not so," Kelly said. "The whole biblical picture of Satan is that of a bad cop to Yaweh's good cop in the Old Testament, and Jesus' good cop in the New Testament. Throughout, Satan is someone who works for God." Professor Kelly has a very interesting viewpoint. But to end this chapter I want to ask a few questions. If he does exist can he truly harm us? No, not according to scripture.

Chapter Sixteen

THE SERPENT

Let's talk about The Serpent in the Garden of Eden. I had my ideas about this but after reading some quotes from Professor Kelly on this topic I like his research better especially the way he explains his ideas. Professor Henry Ansgar Kelly says, "Nobody in the Old Testament — or, for that matter, in the New Testament either — ever identifies the serpent of Eden with Satan," "The serpent is just the smartest animal, and he's motivated by envy after being jilted by Adam for Eve." Kelly traces the correlation of Satan and the serpent to not long after the New Testament was completed. In his "Dialogue With Trypho," the second-century Christian martyr Justin of Samaria first argued that Satan appeared as a serpent to tempt Adam and Eve to disobey God, according to Kelly. "This is what I call

'The New Biography," Kelly said. "It starts with Justin Martyr, who implicates Satan in the fall of Adam and Eve. By causing Adam and Eve to fall, Satan caused his own fall. "The second step in this new and phony biography comes with Origen, who said, 'No, Satan's first sin was not deceiving Adam and Eve or refusing to go along with God's plan of creating Adam in his own image," Kelly said. "'It was to sin out of pride like the morning star, like Lucifer in the passage from Isaiah.' Turning Satan into God's enemy is a two-step process." A scene in the New Testament's Book of Revelation is often cited today as evidence that Satan was the deceiver of Adam and Eve, but the interpretation stems from a fundamental misunderstanding, Kelly argues. "'That ancient serpent' refers to the giant sea serpent Leviathan, not the garden snake of Eden," he said. "In Revelation, Leviathan has morphed into a dragon, or large serpent, with the seven heads and 10 horns, which is still further removed from the seductive serpent who deceived Eve." In addition to linking Satan with the Garden of Eden, the passage from

Revelation also has been used to prove that Satan fell early on in the Bible, but Kelly insists that is not accurate. "Satan's ouster from Heaven in Revelation is explained as taking place in the future," Kelly said. "In Revelation 12:10, a voice says that 'the accuser of our brothers is cast out, overcome by the testimony of martyrs.' Since there were no martyrs until Christ died, that has to be in the future." I couldn't have said it better, Thanks, Professor Kelly.

Chapter Seventeen

SPIRITUAL WARFARE

For a lot of Christians like myself who were taught about the Devil and his demons in church, spiritual warfare consumes a large part of our life, throughout our day, and most definitely consumes the majority of our prayer time. But is it possible that spiritual warfare is not scriptural at all? The most referenced verse of Scripture used to validate Spiritual Warfare is Ephesians Chapter Six, which talks about wrestling with spiritual wickedness and rulers of darkness in high places. We are gonna break those Scriptures down but let's work our way up to those verses. Please allow me to start in the beginning, in Genesis Chapter Three. God mentioned how the seed of the woman, (speaking of Christ) would come and crush the head of Satan with his heel. Meaning, that Jesus will finish Satan and he did over 2,000 years ago on the cross at Calvary. Colossians Chapter Two, talks about how God through the cross triumphed over Principalities and Powers. Hebrews Chapter Two verse Fourteen, talks about how Christ through his death on the cross destroyed the Devil and his works. First John three and Eight say Jesus destroyed the Devil's works. Now if Jesus, according to all those verses of Scripture, crushed the Devil, disabled him, destroyed him, and finished him, then why are we picking a fight with him? Are we spiritual bullies? Why are we going to war with and beating up on someone who has already been defeated? Is it possible that we are engaging in spiritual warfare with a disabled person? According to Scripture, he can't defend himself, he can't fight back, he can't hurt us, because he has already been defeated by Jesus Christ. So leave the Devil and his demons alone you bully. LOL! Honestly, I've never really considered myself a bully nor have I considered the thought that I was picking fights with the Devil. I always felt like the Devil and his demons were picking fights with me but if I am to trust Scripture and what Christ did on the Cross then maybe I need to come to grips with the idea that I was fighting with someone who was never fighting me back because he simply had no ability to fight back. It reminds me of something that happened to me on my first day at work on the TV show "Empire." a young man named Jerome Griffin walked up to me, he was the Actor Trey Byers stand-in. Jerome began to introduce himself and was very polite and kind and started giving me information on how to be a stand-in and how to behave on set. He said, "If I have any questions, please let him know". He was and still is a very nice guy but some months later I was talking to another stand-in who was new to the show and I explained to them how Jerome had mentored me on my first day, and was the one who helped me and taught me everything. Jerome overheard this and he approached me privately and said to me, he was shocked at what I said about him from my first day. He said, "I thought you didn't like me." He went further to say, "I felt like we had no connection, like there was a disconnect between us, I felt like you didn't like me for some reason." I thought that was odd, because I admired and respected and appreciated everything he had done for me, especially on that first day. I considered him a Godsend and had nothing but great gratitude for him. Jerome and I were in the same place at the same time and seeing the world completely different. For a few days at the beginning, Jerome saw me as adversarial but the only thing in my mind toward him was appreciation and friendship. There is Scripture in Colossians Chapter One verse Twenty-One, that says how "we were enemies with God in our own minds". We assumed and even felt like God was our enemy but that was just in our own minds because, in reality, God was never our enemy. Intriguing to think that it's possible, that the Devil is not now nor has ever been a real threat at all but only in our minds. To you the reader I ask, in consideration of all the evidence we've seen in this book so far, is it possible that if you change your mind about Satan then you could change his ability to affect your life? Think about It. But what about the strongest verses of Scripture in the Bible used to support Spiritual warfare, Ephesians Chapter Six? To look at Ephesians Chapter Six in context we've got to go back to Ephesians Chapter Five. In Chapter Five, The Apostle Paul speaks on how a married couple's relationship is not just physical but spiritual. In context, Paul is talking about how all of our relationships with people are not just physical but spiritual, and how we relate to people is how we relate to God since He is a spirit, we are a spirit and our relationships are spiritual. As we move into Ephesians Chapter Six, talks about how children's relationships with their parents are not just physical but spiritual; he even mentions how our relationships with our persecutors or enemies are not just physical but spiritual. We are wrestling with individuals or better worded, people who have stepped into the role of the Satan or the Opposer, the one who persecutes or brings tribulation upon you. Maybe one of the reasons a lot of us Christians believe that the Devil can do physical harm to us is because we see Scriptures like this that explain how the Devil or the Satan is persecuting people, throwing them in jail, murdering people, and instead of recognizing or realizing that the Bible is clearly talking about literal people or humans doing these things and not an evil spiritual being. By assuming and believing that the Devil is doing this to people in the Bible and because we begin to believe a demon can do that to us as well, we start to allow demons to physically harm and attack us because we believe it. Remember, the Bible says, "Be it unto you according to your faith". What do you believe? According to Scripture, the Devil can not do those things to us, and almost every time the Devil or Satan is mentioned in Scripture it is talking about a literal person or people. Once again, I'm not saying there isn't a literal Devil or Satan, I'm just stating the facts that you can research for yourself. Almost whenever the Devil or Satan is mentioned in Scripture, it is talking about a literal person or people. Not a supernatural, spiritual, evil being. I encourage you to research for yourself. Someone reading this might be thinking, William, even if you are correct that Ephesians Chapter Five and the beginning of Ephesians Chapter Six are talking about literal people, and Chapter Six verses Eleven through Seventeen are talking about demons. It reads, "Put on the full armor of God, that ye may be able to stand against the wiles of the Devil because we wrestle not against flesh and blood but against Principalities, Powers, Spiritual Wickedness in high places and Rulers of Darkness." That sounds like demons to me, William. My reply is if we simply move back just one verse to verse Ten. It starts with the word "finally", meaning this comes after other statements in which this one is connected. Consider the fact that if the verses before this are talking about literal people then the ones we're talking about now in context have to still be talking about literal people. This is simply a continuation and a conclusion of the previous Chapters. I think that the scriptural context I just addressed is compelling enough but allow me to mention the fact that there were no chapters and verses in the original writings. This was a simple letter written to the Church in Corinth, which adds even more confirmation to the context of this chapter. Let's go deeper into these verses, to attempt to confirm this point. The Scripture says, "We wrestle against Principalities" The literal biblical definition of Principalities means a State ruled by a Prince, (a literal person, an actual Son of a King) also check out the root word of Principalities. That word is "principles", meaning ways of thinking. Next, it says, we wrestle against Powers. Powers simply means people in power. Consider this popular phrase that uses this same word, "The Powers that be". Again, talking about literal people in power. The literal Greek definition of Powers means, "your rights, your authority or your tokens of control." The things we think we control or have rights to own or have rights to control are the Powers referred to in this verse. Could the early church at the beginning of Christianity have been feeling threatened by the control or beliefs of people in positions of power? Absolutely! History repeatedly confirms that fact through many documents of Church history and so does the Bible. Regarding the rest of the verse, can Rulers of Darkness and Spiritual Wickedness in high places, simply be referring to Governors,

Mayors, Kings, Scribes, and Pharisees? Bible stories as well as Secular History report that people in power persecuted and were at odds with the early church for many years, even murdering them, in horrible ways. Maybe we've been imagining that the Scripture is saying something that it simply is not. Please keep in mind that I have not been giving you "Second William Chapter Two." I have been using the Bible to clarify the Bible. Think about it, pray about it, and study for yourself. I try not to tell people what to think or how to believe. I used to do that all the time while Preaching or Teaching the Bible when I was younger. These days I prefer to allow you to come to your own conclusion which is why I ask so many questions as opposed to telling you what is true or false. Is it possible that the Principalities, powers, etc. that Scripture says, we fight or wrestle against, are simply the ideas propagated by people, especially people in power? Could Scripture mean that we wrestle against schemes, lies, tricks, false beliefs, and evil imaginations of people in positions of authority and people in general? Maybe the

Apostle Paul was warning us that we don't fight against people but against people's beliefs. Was he saying that our fight is a spiritual fight? Growing up in Church, I was taught to be afraid of speaking my plans or my goals out loud because the Devil could not hear the thoughts I had in my mind but if I said it out loud then he could hatch a plan to try to stop my dreams, visions and my goals. So I never spoke my plans out loud. On occasion when I forgot and did speak my plans out loud or what I wanted to accomplish, true to form or just as expected, something always went wrong. Something always happened to hinder me from doing or achieving what I said I was gonna do. So the spiritual warfare would begin. My life was a constant fight, a continuous struggle with evil forces. I woke up every morning, putting on the Full Armor of God, to prepare for battle. That was not a life of peace, but a life of war. Now some of you reading this love to battle more than peace or love warfare more than peace and I understand that because fighting can help us to not feel like victims so battling can sometimes feel like the better solution. But if you want to have some peace. If you are tired of wrestling or fighting with the Devil, your liberation or freedom is in this book. It's also in the Bible as we discovered by a simple studying of the Scriptures in context, void of man's opinion on the Scriptures. If you long for peace and freedom from Spiritual Warfare, you can have it today, right now! Speaking personally, I now wake up every morning speaking out loud about what I will accomplish today or what my life plans, dreams, and goals are without any fear or concerns about them being hindered by the Devil or his demons. And they are never hindered, Please believe it. I've learned that one of my greatest weapons for success has been the ability to speak out loud about what I want to accomplish. I speak my dreams and goals like the Scripture says, "To speak those things that be not as though they were". Another verse says, "You shall have what you say". For many years I allowed the Devil to hinder me from speaking my life into existence, I allowed lies and misunderstandings to make me think that if I did attempt to speak the life I wanted into existence he would defeat my goals and plans. Is it possible that the Devil is weak and can't do anything unless you believe he can? Maybe we should repent which simply means to change our minds and change the way we think about the Devil. Can changing your mind about Satan change his power in your life? As far as I'm concerned the Devil is nothing to me. I'm not wasting my time giving that fool any attention. He does not deserve to be a part of my day! The Devil is defeated and honestly according to Scripture if you want to wrestle and fight the Devil in spiritual warfare then in essence you are saying that Jesus was a failure, that He didn't already defeat the Devil, that Christ's sacrifice on the Cross for us was useless as far as defeating Satan was concerned. Is our fear, struggle, or warfare with the Devil confirmation that we don't trust in Jesus Christ or God the Father? Maybe we could spend more time in prayer getting to know our Heavenly Father and getting to know ourselves as opposed to wrestling the Devil and his demons in spiritual warfare. Maybe we can begin to take more responsibility for our actions as opposed to blaming the Devil and his demons for everything. Maybe it'll be easier to forgive people by realizing that it's their ideas, their beliefs, and their principles that these people have that can cause them to be at odds with us as opposed to the person. Maybe if we could affect their beliefs or we could change their viewpoint, it would allow them to see things from our viewpoint or a different side altogether. Let it marinate.

Chapter Eighteen

HELL &

THE ETERNAL TEASE

I remember reading this true story that scared the Hell out of me, about a Mother by the Name of Andrea Yates from Texas who in 2001 drowned her five young children in the bathtub to prevent them from suffering in hell before they became the age of accountability. The oldest of her five children she drowned to death was only Seven years old. During her trial, she pleaded insanity and was found Not Guilty. It was reported that her Pastor after years of counseling informed her and her husband that they were destined for hell. After a nervous breakdown and two suicide attempts Mrs. Yates believed she was damaging her children and it would be better to kill them and herself than to allow her young children to get old enough to follow her example and go to hell with her. She told her jail psychiatrist that her children were doomed to perish in the fires of Hell because she was their mother and a bad example to them. So she had to kill them before they reached the age of accountability. (There is a supposed age of accountability where children aren't held accountable until they reach this age. That specific age differs depending on who states it. But there is no scriptural confirmation or validation for this age of accountability nor the imagined consequences.) Andrea Yates believed murdering her five young children saved them from eternal torture in the fire pits of Hell. Sadly this is not the only occurrence of such beliefs or actions.

Would a Loving and Compassionate God create a fire that never dies, then design that fire to burn the flesh from the bones of His Children? Would He create it to last for just one full day? Would our Loving and Compassionate Heavenly Father design it to burn people for just a month? Imagine Him designing it to torture and burn your flesh for ten years, one hundred years, or as taught in many churches, for All Eternity? A place where His children, your brother/sister or Your Child will suffer and be tormented in ways too horrible to imagine, Forever? Hell No! Or maybe the undeniable truth is Hell Yes! We will get into it in this chapter.

Several years ago, I think it was 2013 or earlier when I was still living in Detroit. I remember trying to change my view of life. I had a lot of negative thoughts. I continually saw a lot of sadness and fear in my life, it was a very stressful time and I was trying, as the Scriptures instruct us to, "Set my affections on things above, not on things on the earth". I was rededicating my commitment to God and taking the Bible more seriously. I was attempting to, as the Bible says, "Think on those things which are lovely, which are pure, which are of any virtue, of any praise, think on these things". My Pastor at that time was Reginald R. Lane of Dunamis Outreach Ministries and he had just mentioned in a

Sermon one Sunday morning that we should do those same things, even stating those same Scriptures so that was all the confirmation I needed. I made up my mind that I was going to do just that. I was going to start changing the way I saw things, and the way I thought. So the first thing that came to my mind was to set my affections on things above like Heaven, so I decided that I was going to look up every Scripture in the Bible on Heaven and start focusing on them, memorizing them, and meditating on them to get them in my spirit, so I can become more Heavenly Minded. But something strange and unexpected was being revealed to me as I researched all the Scriptures from Genesis to Revelation on Heaven. Every Scripture, every verse, one after the other that mentioned Heaven, the Kingdom of Heaven, or the Kingdom of God. I was shocked to realize that nearly every instance in scripture was talking about a place on Earth or inside of us, not in the sky above the clouds. The Legendary Pearly Gates are on Earth. The New Jerusalem is on Earth. When the Bible talks about The Wolf living with the Lamb is on

Earth. A Child lying down with the Leopard is also on Earth. Now this one really caught me off guard. According to Scripture, the famous and often preached about Heavenly "Streets Paved with Gold" are located on Earth as well. All of the preached about Heavenly Peace and Joy is also located on Earth, inside of ourselves according to scripture. Research it for yourself. Do as I did and get your Greek translations, your Hebrew translations, Strong's concordance, Vine's expository, etc, and discover the truth for yourself. I'm not trying to convince you of anything. I'm simply telling you something that happened to me. I went there in search of Scriptures about Heaven in an attempt to uplift my thought patterns, to uplift the way I saw things, to have a paradigm shift, to think on good things, and to set my affection on things above, not on things on the earth. I wanted to as the Bible says, think of those things which are pure, which are lovely, and are of a good report. My logical mind figured, how could I go any higher than Heaven and I came to discover in my research that it appears that almost every verse of Scripture that mentions Heaven, the Kingdom of God, or the Kingdom of Heaven is talking about a state of being, a mindset or a literal place on earth.

A friend of mine who once studied to become a Priest said that he was told in Catechism class that Heaven is a way of being. He was taught Heaven is not a place but is in our minds. According to the Catholic Answers website. Heaven is within us, in the sense that each Christian is a temple of the indwelling Trinity. But it is no more accurate to say that heaven is only within us than it is to say that, by virtue of our receiving the sacraments, Jesus exists only within us. God and heaven live within us—but they also have an objective life beyond us as well. God, in a sense, is heaven. In 1 Maccabees 3:18, for example, the author uses "Heaven" as a name for God (to avoid using the name it was forbidden to pronounce). Heaven exists wherever God is. Jesus said, "The kingdom of heaven is at hand" (Matthew 4:17), meaning that, since God took on flesh, heaven itself is here, among us. After death, our experience of heaven will be to enter fully into the intimate love of the Holy Trinity, to our everlasting and perfect joy. To the extent that we participate in that love while on earth, we begin to share the joy of heaven now. The Bible refers to "heavenly places." We must keep in mind that time and space are finite concepts; God is not bound by them, nor could God live in one physical place, as we think of it because the physical universe is his creation and cannot contain him. Heaven is a place, but not a particular space. We must understand the symbolic language of the Bible and the saints as an attempt to communicate the ineffable. We do not understand literary terms such as seeing God "face to face." We rejoice in their meaning: that we will be with God, intimate with him, unhindered by our mortal limitations.

As the Catechism says (section 1024), "This perfect life with the Most Holy Trinity—this communion of life and love with the Trinity, with the Virgin Mary, the angels and all the blessed—is called 'heaven.' Heaven is the ultimate end and fulfillment of the deepest human longings, the state of supreme, definitive happiness." Am I saying that there is not a Heaven up in the sky where God dwells? I don't know if there is or not, there could be, I'm not here to debate that, nor am I here to disprove that. I honestly don't know but I can say that you can research this for yourself and you will see that most of the Scriptures in the Bible that are talking about Heaven are not talking about some place up in the sky where God lives. There are only an extremely small few scriptures that in context can allude to a possible place in the sky after death. The Bible says that God and the Kingdom of Heaven live on the inside of us. Look it up, check it out for yourself. So now what does that mean about Hell? If Heaven is a literal state of being or mindset that we can acquire here on this earth, does that mean Hell is the same? Is the God of Love so evil as to create an eternal place of damnation and torment but only have Heaven on earth? Maybe. Let's get into it. Almost every religion throughout human history has some idea of a horrible life after death. Even though the threat of fire and brimstone is not preached as strongly today as it used to be during medieval times. It's not even preached today as forcefully as it was preached in the late 70s when I first started attending church. Yet, It is still very hard for modern believers and their religious institutions to let go of the medieval vision of Hell. Is the God of Love as He is called in Scripture, willing to burn people for all eternity without ever totally burning them up? Is He willing to horribly torture your unsaved Mother or your unsaved Son forever? Apart from what you believe the Scriptures teach, ask yourself, what kind of God is capable of this? Would the loving God of the Bible, design a never-ending torture chamber? How enjoyable could heaven be for us if we were forced to watch our children or parents and other loved ones, screaming in pain and agony for the rest of time? Is that a real heaven? Can you see the absurdity of this idea? Yet millions of people, myself included, come to this conclusion when we accept the beliefs surrounding the popular concept of Hell. The Encyclopedia says, "Hell is the abode of evil spirits; the infernal regions…where lost and condemned souls go after death to suffer indescribable torments and eternal punishment...Some have thought of it as the place created by the Deity, where He punishes with inconceivable severity, and through all eternity, the souls of those who through unbelief or the worship of false Gods have angered Him. It is the place of divine revenge, untempered, never-ending." WOW! Although this view of Hell is widely believed to be in Scripture, I challenge you to search the Bible and find anything even in the vicinity of these horrors. You would have to use your imagination to a great degree to find anything similar in the Scriptures. Did you know that this popular worldwide view of Hell originated from a very famous Pagan Poem? Dante Alighieri's born in 1265 and died in 1321. Had a famous work called The Divine Comedy. In it, he wrote a poem describing his vision of Hell called "Dante's Inferno". Dante was fascinated with and got his ideas from the pagan philosophers Plato and Virgil. The fact of the matter is that the concept of an ever-burning Hell comes from outright paganism, not the Bible! Now let's address Hell in the Scriptures.

John 3:16 states, "For God so loved the world, that He gave His only begotten Son, that whosoever believes in Him should not perish, but have everlasting life." Those who receive salvation are promised that they "should not perish" but "have eternal life!" If Hell is a place of eternal torture, then the people suffering this torment must also have eternal life, right? But the verse says, "should not perish." It does not say, "Should not suffer eternal life in torment." Romans 6:23: "For the wages of sin is death, but the gift of God is eternal life through Jesus Christ our Lord." This verse exactly mirrors John 3:16! Eternal life is contrasted to death, to perishing. The wages of sin is death, not eternal torture in Hell. God says He pays the wicked a paycheck with wages of death, not life in a place of torture. The Bible mentions Hell in numerous passages. The Bible uses three Greek words in the New Testament, and one Hebrew word in the Old Testament, explaining the meaning of Hell. Let's examine these words.

Sheol: The Hebrew word translated as Hell in the Old Testament is sheol. It has a New

Testament counterpart, hades. Actually, if you look up sheol in a concordance, it will reference the Greek word hades. They both mean "the grave, pit, world of the dead or Hell." Hell is the tomb. Scripture does state that all people do go to "Hell" at death! Since the Bible does say, "It is appointed unto men once to die" (Heb. 9:27), then everyone does die and go to Hell— literally. All people eventually go to the grave.

Hades: Hades is the most common word used in the New Testament for "Hell." Virtually all sources agree that sheol and hades are the same and that both refer to the grave.

Tartaros: Tartaros is the second Greek word translated as "Hell". It is found only once in the New Testament. In II Peter 2:4: "For if God spared not the angels that sinned, but cast them down to Hell, and delivered them into chains of darkness, to be reserved unto judgment." It means "a prison, incarceration, place of restraint or a dark abyss." This verse doesn't reference humans but describes the imprisoning of the angels on Earth as their "place of restraint" or "prison" after their rebellion.

Gehenna: Gehenna is the final Greek word translated as Hell or Hell Fire in the New Testament.   Hasting's Dictionary says, "The word Gehenna occurs twelve times in the New Testament. This term 'gehenna' represents 'the Valley of Hinnom' (Neh. 11:30, II Kings 23:10, etc.). The place was…a deep narrow gorge in the vicinity of Jerusalem, understood to be on the south side. It is repeatedly mentioned in the Old Testament (Jer. 19:6, etc.). It became an object of horror to the Jews and is said to have been made the receptacle for bones, the bodies of beasts and criminals, refuse, and all unclean things. The terrible associations of the place…the fires said to have been kept burning in it to consume the foul and corrupt objects that were thrown into it, made it [an]…unmistakable symbol of dire evil…absolute ruin. So it came to designate the place of future punishment." This is a real place near Jerusalem and looks just as described. You can go see it for yourself. Some of the bodies that were cast into this valley never made it into the fires burning below. They would get hung up in the brush and trees on the ledges near the rim. In describing the wicked, when Christ stated that "their worms die not," He was referring to the bodies of certain criminals that were thrown over the edge of the ravine but did not burn up because they got stuck on a ledge. They literally rotted and decomposed where they were. The maggots that entered their bodies completed the decomposition process without interruption from either the fire or anything else. These worms "died not," so to speak, because they later developed into flies. This graphic picture is part of the reason that Gehenna was such a place of revulsion to all who were familiar with it!

<u>The Lake of Fire:</u> The Valley of Hinnom—Gehenna—came to represent a place of final punishment—a place of "absolute ruin"—for all who go there. The reference to Hellfire refers to the "lake of fire" described in Revelation 20:13-15: "And the sea gave up the dead which was in it, and death and

Hell delivered up the dead which was in them: and they were judged every man according to their works. And death and Hell [hades] were cast into the lake of fire. This is the second death. And whosoever was not found written in the book of life was cast into the lake of fire."

All who enter this lake suffer permanent death. They suffer complete destruction—a final and everlasting punishment—eternal—permanent! It is not punishing but is rather the everlasting punishment. The eternal punishment is a one-time thing, not continuous or repetitive. Jude 7 speaks of the ancient cities of Sodom and Gomorrah having received the "vengeance of eternal fire" for their sins. Those cities are not burning today. Their destruction was eternal. When those cities completely burned up, the fires went out. However, their punishment continues to this day! In Jeremiah 17:27 and 52:13. God warned Jerusalem that He would burn her with an "unquenchable fire," if she did not repent. That "Unquenchable Fire" happened but Jerusalem is not still burning today.

Everlasting Punishment: MATTHEW 25:41, 46: "Then shall He say also unto them on the left hand, Depart from Me, you cursed, into everlasting fire, prepared for the Devil and his angels...And these shall go away into everlasting punishment: but the righteous into life eternal." Is this proof of an ever-burning Hell? It is not! The Greek word, aionios (from which comes the English word eon), translated "everlasting," means "age lasting." An Age is a designated period of time that comes to an end.

The biggest rebuttal I face if I mention the possibility that Hell might not be real is the fact that Jesus Christ mentioned it more than He did about Heaven Jesus mentioned Hell more than anyone else in the whole canon of scripture. But again the original word used by Jesus is Gehenna which is an actual location that can be seen today in Jerusalem. In biblical times it was called Gei Ben-Hinnom which means the Valley of the Son of Hinnom or Gei-Hinnom.

This is very interesting. Check this out. Webster's dictionary explains that the word or term hell originated from old English and high German beginning in the Anglo-Saxon period of 400 AD to 1100 AD. Our word helmet has the same origins. They both mean to cover or conceal. In the Middle Ages, potato farmers would hell their potatoes. Meaning they would bury them under dirt to preserve them during the winter. According to historical documents from the Middle Ages, those farmers referred to the process of burying their potatoes to protect them as "placing them in hel". "Helliers" were people who covered homes with roofs for protection from the elements. So according to the origins of the word hell, we are putting people in hell every time we bury them by covering the bodies to protect them from exposure. Even closing the casket lid can be considered helling or covering someone. This is not attached to suffering in any way, it's attached to protection and safety. Maybe we are adding our own ideas and taught beliefs to scriptures that in all honesty don't mean what we assume. Let it marinate.

Psalms 136:2 & 26 says that "God's mercy endures forever." Forever means forever or for all eternity. It doesn't say His mercy lasts till we die and go to hell, it endures forever.

This contradicts the Hell Forever message in my opinion.

God loves you Unconditionally Unless you don't confess Jesus Christ as your personal Lord and Savior. So, you can be a good person but because you don't accept Jesus as your Savior then God who loves us unconditionally will sentence us to suffer torture in the Lake of Fire Forever? Seems kinda schizophrenic, doesn't it? Unconditional means, not subject to any conditions, no conditions whatsoever. Let it marinate.

Romans 8:38-39 King James Version states, "For I am persuaded, that neither death, nor life, nor angels, nor principalities, nor powers, nor things present, nor things to come, Nor height, nor depth, nor any other creature, shall be able to separate us from the love of God, which is in Christ Jesus our Lord." Many define Hell as separation from

126

the love of God but according to the bible, separation from the Love of God is impossible. If according to scripture not even death can separate us from God and His love for us then I believe this is another contradiction to the idea of burning in hell for all eternity.

For over 40 years I looked forward to a wonderful place in the afterlife, a sweet bye-and-bye where I would finally find Peace. I believed that in this world I'd go through turmoil and pain but one day Jesus is going to come back to get me and take me to Heaven or I would die and go to Heaven. Then I'll be at Peace, then I'll live in Joy and then I'll finally be Happy. I lived every day looking and thinking about that glorious day when I get to Heaven but is it possible that I missed the boat? Is it possible that I could have been in Heaven all along, that I can currently live in Heaven right now on Earth, in this body? Could I have wasted time waiting for that sweet bye-and-bye? Is it possible that you can be in Heaven right now? Could it be simply a mindset or a way of thinking that places us in either Heaven or Hell? Scripture says that the Kingdom of Heaven is Righteousness, Peace, and Joy. Can you have that right now? I can't speak for you but I can tell you that there are times when I am thinking correctly that I feel like I'm in Heaven. I've been feeling that way for the last few years. There are many times I feel like I'm in Heaven on Earth, I feel like Heaven is in me! I can feel like I'm in complete ecstasy at times. I've never been this Joyous, I've never had this much Peace, I've never had this much Security, I've never felt this intimate, close, and loving relationship with God as I do right now. Is it possible that if you're living in Hell right now you're choosing to? Is it possible that it is only a state of mind? If you feel like you are in Hell, is it possible that you can choose to repent, which means changing your mind and thinking differently? Maybe you can change your thinking and all of a sudden you're in Heaven. Maybe you can put yourself in Heaven. The Holy Bible seems to confirm this possibility. Scripture says, cast down every thought and every imagination that exalts itself against the knowledge of God. It says we should think on those things which are lovely, pure, of any virtue or any praise, we should think on those things. Another verse of Scripture says as a man thinketh in his heart, so is he. If you think you are in Heaven, are you automatically in Heaven? If you think you are in Hell, are you automatically in Hell? Again I was not seeking to disprove that there was a Heaven after I died, I only looked with a sincere goal of trying to grow, change, and have a paradigm shift, so I can start viewing life from a more optimistic viewpoint. I was pleasantly surprised to learn that it was possible, Heaven could be mine right now. Heaven can be yours right now! If there is a Heaven after we die or not, who cares? I'm done feeding anxiety in my life, worrying about what happens after I die. I've done that for over 40 years and it brought me nothing but stress and misery in the moment unless I felt my life was good enough at that moment to warrant going to Heaven as opposed to Hell. Joy, Peace, and Happiness in a future Heaven after death felt like an Eternal Tease. One day, in the sweet by and by, I'll be okay but right now I'm suffering. I'd rather be in Heaven right now in this lifetime, how about you? Search the Scriptures for yourself. Make up your own mind. Pray about it, and use your common sense Christianity to decide for yourself.

Please allow me to take this opportunity to make a public Apology, to a Wonderful Man of God who I feel I betrayed many years ago. He doesn't personally know me but we've been in each other's presence on a couple of occasions. Because he denied the existence of Hell many years ago, I denounced him and criticized him publicly. So I want to Apologize publicly. There was a very popular Preacher from Tulsa Oklahoma named Bishop Carlton Pearson. I was a huge fan of his Ministry. I watched his Television broadcasts regularly, read his books, and listened to his music because he was a great singer as well. I had even gone to see him live a couple of times. His Azuza meetings in the '90s were legendary! In the early 2000's I believe it was, he began saying some very controversial things like, he believed that Jehovah's

Witnesses, Muslims, and Buddhists are saved just like us Christians. Now let me admit that the details of what Bishop Carlton Pearson said might be off some because they were reported to me by second-hand knowledge or hearsay from my Church family and other Preachers on radio and TV. There was an uproar about this in the Body of Christ. Christians at least in my Church circles thought he had lost his mind. I remember having heated debates after this news came out because I was already a controversial believer and I thought what he was saying had some validity. I had already been saying similar things myself. So I defended him repeatedly and proudly. That is until I was informed he made a statement that Hell did not exist. I couldn't believe it. That statement was so preposterous in my mind that I couldn't take people's word for that, I had to go see if it was true myself. I was flabbergasted, he did indeed say that. Although I didn't go to the extremes of calling him a Heretic, a Crazy fool, or the AntiChrist as a lot of Christians did. I felt that I could no longer defend him. He had clearly in my opinion lost his mind. Before this,

Pastor Pearson had hit Gospel Records, a Worldwide Traveling Ministry, and a huge Church with over 6,000 members. After he made the statement about there being no Hell, I was told his ministry dwindled to a few dozen members renting out a small hall to hold church services. I could only imagine what other horrible things happened to him after that. Religious folks can be extremely cruel, hateful, and even violent, especially if we think we are on the opposite side of God or the Bible. I believed Bishop Pearson to be very intelligent and accurate in knowing the Scriptures. I considered myself very Bible-educated and I didn't find myself correcting his teachings as I was known to do often to other Preachers. Yet I still wasn't wise enough to sit down and study his viewpoint. I simply abandoned him publicly and would state if asked about him, that he has indeed lost his mind! He had earned enough respect to be at least listened to and fully understood before being cast aside by me. I wish I had behaved more maturely, better yet more Christ-like. Bishop Carlton Pearson, I sincerely apologize for not respecting you enough to at least research your viewpoint before immaturely abandoning you. I sincerely Apologize for my actions! I was wrong!

As I write this apology I am reminded of a point Apostle Pearson made about Adolf Hitler. It went something like this, Hitler is hated and despised by many on the planet as being one of the most evil leaders to have ever lived. Hitler sentenced thousands of people to be gassed and then burned in mass graves after death with a fire that maybe lasted for mere minutes but God on the other hand can sentence Billions of people to burn after death for not just a few hours but for all eternity and is considered Just and Good. Something seems off with this logic. Maybe we have misunderstood God and the Bible.

The kingdom of God is a central concept in the teachings of Jesus. But is it possible that it refers to the reign and rule of God on earth in our hearts and minds? Scriptures state, it is a place of peace, love, and justice, where God's will is done and his glory is revealed. Is it possible that the kingdom of God is a spiritual reality that can be experienced by anyone who seeks it? Sometimes I enjoy reading religious books without being inundated with a bunch of scriptures but I understand that I feel that way because I have been studying the Bible for many years and I usually know when someone is saying something that is not backed by scripture but I am also aware that I am saying some controversial things that some people are not going to believe unless I show scriptures so I am going to give a few of the scriptures on the Kingdom of Heaven or the Kingdom of God at the end of this chapter and if you are versed in the bible then you can already confirm what I'm saying is true and can simply skip to the next chapter.

Otherwise, check out how these scriptures talk about the Kingdom of Heaven.

Verses like this next one smacked me in the mouth and were very hard for me to ignore. It was honestly embarrassing. Reading this first verse in context it is clear that the Kingdom had to have already come unless we are led to believe that there are people still alive waiting on it over 2000 years later. Impossible!

Mark 9:1 And he said to them, "Truly, I say to you, there are some standing here who will not taste death until they see the kingdom of God after it has come with power."

This one hit me hard as well.

Luke 17:20-21   Being asked by the Pharisees when the kingdom of God would come, he answered them, "The kingdom of God is not coming in ways that can be observed, nor will they say, 'Look, here it is!' or 'There!' for behold, the kingdom of God is in the midst of you."

Matthew 6:33 "But seek first his kingdom and his righteousness, and all these things will be given to you as well."

Romans 14:17 "For the kingdom of God is not a matter of eating and drinking, but of righteousness, peace and joy in the Holy Spirit."

Matthew 21:43 "Therefore, I tell you, the kingdom of God will be taken away from you and given to a people who will produce its fruit."

Mark 1:15 The time is fulfilled, and the kingdom of God is at hand; repent and believe in the gospel.

Matthew 9:35 And Jesus went throughout all the cities and villages, teaching in their synagogues and proclaiming the gospel of the kingdom and healing every disease and every affliction.

Matthew 12:28 But if it is by the Spirit of God that I drive out demons, then the kingdom of God has come upon you.

Matthew 13:31-33 The kingdom of heaven is like a mustard seed, which a man took and planted in his field. Though it is the smallest of all seeds, yet when it grows, it is the largest of garden plants and becomes a tree, so that the birds come and perch in its branches. He told them another parable. "The kingdom of heaven is like leaven that a woman took and hid in three measures of flour, till it was all leavened."

Matthew 13:44-46 The kingdom of heaven is like treasure hidden in a field, which a man found and covered up. Then in his joy, he goes and sells all that he has and buys that field. Again, the kingdom of heaven is like a merchant in search of fine pearls, who, on finding one pearl of great value, went and sold all that he had and bought it.

Romans 14:17 For the kingdom of God is not a matter of eating and drinking but of righteousness and peace and joy in the Holy Spirit.

1 Corinthians 4:20 For the kingdom of God does not consist in talk but in power.

This next one sounds like a past tense verse of scripture to me.

Colossians 1:13 He has delivered us from the domain of darkness and transferred us to the kingdom of his beloved Son.

Let's be clear according to the scriptures in context. Heaven, the Kingdom of God, the Kingdom of Heaven, and, the Gospel of the Kingdom are all talking about the same thing.

Heaven is a place I believe can be found in our hearts and minds. There are too many verses to display them all and to have to explain them all. This isn't that type of book but I encourage you to do your own study. Please don't just read the scriptures on Heaven, read them in context so you will have a more complete picture. As I've stated in other chapters. My goal is to give you some things to think about and I trust that you will pray about it, research it, and use your common sense Christianity to realize your truth. Be it unto you according to your faith.

Chapter Nineteen

THE STING OF DEATH

I s it possible that Death is only bad because we view it as such? Mankind has sought the world over for a fountain of youth and a way to evade death out of fear. Let's imagine for a moment the state this world would be in if we didn't have the gift of death. If mankind could live forever the earth would quickly be overpopulated. Do you think the earth would have accomplished or created as much as it has if we knew we would live forever? How important would it be to create or accomplish things? How many truths and healing conversations would be hidden for eternity? A sad fact of life is how, many people never find out the truth of who their real father is until someone is at the edge of death. How often in this life do people finally reunite with a long-lost friend or family member only because people recognize their immortality? People have an urge to create things or contribute to society before they pass from this world. All of that would likely end if we lived forever on this planet. We would likely take life for granted even more than we do already while thinking we have a good 70 years to live. People may have goals to start their books or their inventions after the age of 500 years old for example. What's the rush? Examine people around you and you may notice those that are more in tune with the limited amount of time we have on this earth. Those who are more in tune with how Scripture states that tomorrow is promised to no man are usually more diligent and more productive and accomplish more with a greater impact on our society because they are aware that life is short. A bonus is that usually those people are more content in life and enjoy each day more than those of us who ignore the fragility of life.

Death, Fear, Anxiety, and Pain are all wonderful blessings to us. Consider a Baseball bat. It has been used in the United States to bring entertainment, exercise, sport, competition, protection, and wealth to millions of people for decades. But another fact is that Baseball bats have been used to wound, maim, and murder people for just as long. The bat is not the problem, it's how it's used that can cause an issue.

Fear is a gift that can warn us to avoid imminent danger, like wild animals, etc. Anxiety can cause us to prepare ourselves and our families to avoid danger or suffering. Pain allows us to know when something is wrong with us that we may not ever notice otherwise. I've heard of a man who could not feel pain burning his hand beyond repair because he didn't realize he was on fire. But any of these gifts can cause us to suffer if they are misused or overused.

Maybe if we dispose of the dread of death, it can cause us to be more appreciative of life as a whole. When I was about 13, some chemical fell into my eyes from the roof of a building and I lost my eyesight for a brief time. After I regained my sight and until this day I can randomly have a loving appreciation for my eyesight. My eyesight was never important before that. Until I started losing my hair, it wasn't valued. I wore my hair bald for over a year just to save money but when I became aware that I no longer had any choice, every moment with even a little hair was appreciated. Have you noticed how people born into money don't usually appreciate it but if you've been poor, then money means so much more to you? Maybe bad things happening is a blessing and a gift from God or the Universe? Pain from a hot stove warning us to remove our hands is a blessing. A toothache, warning us to avoid letting our teeth rot out of our mouths, etc. Maybe it's all a simple matter of perspective. Life teaches us that dealing with painful things is the best way to be healed in life. Think about how therapists deal directly with your pain and they try to hold you there in that painful memory till you are free from it. Likewise, a physical therapist does the same with our physical pain. Say you hurt your shoulder, the doctor or therapist will have you doing things with your shoulder on purpose during the recovery process that often hurts more than just leaving it alone. But the truth is the therapy both mentally and physically will heal you so that the pain never returns. On the other hand, ignoring it can cause us to suffer the injury or pain to linger for our entire life. Could pain or things we consider bad or evil truly be a simple perspective that we can change at will?

Chapter Twenty

THE ESSENCE OF EVIL

There is possibly something we could learn from the Marvel Comic Book characters, Killmonger and Thanos. I want to bring an idea to you today and allow you to judge for yourself to see if it has any validity. Consider this, if God is omnipresent, that means He is everywhere at the same time right? If God is love and is everywhere at the same time then how can evil truly exist? Where can it exist, if God is everywhere? You can pile the maximum amount of darkness in one area as much as you can fit and it will always lose to the smallest flicker of light. Light always wins. Where there is light, darkness no longer exists. There is no competition, no struggle, and no battle, darkness dies in the presence of light, always. For darkness to exist there has to be no light, but if God is love and light and he is everywhere, at all times then where and how can darkness or evil truly exist? Is it possible that people we might consider evil are more like Thanos and Killmonger? Thanos wiped out half the population of the galaxy but in his mind it was for the greater good, likewise, Killmonger killed and wanted to start a war to kill more people but in his mind, it was all for the greater good. Was he really a bad guy? Is it possible that everyone who does something that we might consider evil is truly acting from a place of their understanding, their beliefs, ways they were raised, ideas, and actions that make complete sense to them? Now let me be clear, I'm not saying that these things that we may deem as evil, should not be dealt with. Both Killmonger and Thanos were destroyed because of their actions. When we are dealing with people whose actions in this world seem hurtful to us, when it feels like they are attacking us, and in our pain it could appear like they are just straight-up evil. Could it be possible that they are simply surviving as best they can? Could they be wounded or damaged themselves and consider attacking you a better way to live as opposed to remaining a victim themselves? I've learned from years of counseling that there are individuals who have only known pain and suffering in their life so consequently that is all they know how to give. I'm sure you know someone like that. You can compliment them and they take it as an insult, you can give them a gift and they think you want something from them and if you do something nice for them they are suspicious and think you are trying to trick them somehow.

They have become comfortable living like that. Maybe it's not always as intentionally evil as we feel it to be. We might be able to solve more issues or come to terms with and understand peoples' actions better if we put a little more energy into trying to understand why so and so is doing this or that as opposed to just chalking them up as being evil or just bad people. As a young man, people who hurt or wounded me, I naturally viewed them as simply evil and at times completely unforgivable but as I've matured, I gained the ability to place myself in other people's shoes. I try to look at it from their viewpoint, from their understanding and to simply ask questions, instead of assuming why he or she said or did something hurtful to me. Being able to do that has completely shifted how I viewed those things I considered atrocities towards me in my past. Again, I'm not saying that they were ok or they were right to do it. Nor am I saying, I deserved it. I am saying that personally from being the victim or the observer of what I considered evil, I mentally placed a label on them and put them in a category of enemy or evil but with wisdom and sometimes just conversation I was able to see that evil or even evil intent was not involved. After listening to some of my villains explain their actions, often it made complete logical sense to them what they were doing or they considered it as a lesser of two evils at times. Many different examples from my memories are flooding my mind as I write this but I don't want to tell people's business, especially since we are in a healed state currently and that's not necessarily the purpose of this Chapter anyway. What they did was wrong! It was painful and damaging but they all had reasons that made absolute sense from their viewpoints. Just like you and I have likely wounded people and they think of us as being evil but we knew that it made sense to us, we were not trying to hurt anybody, we were doing what we thought was good for our survival in the situation. You may be at odds with somebody right now from 30 years ago and you see it one way and they see it an entirely different way. Ask them and I bet they view you as the villain but you're looking at them like they are the villain. No doubt in your mind, you can justify what you did. Does true evil really exist? Is it even possible to exist? Maybe it does, I don't know, I'm not trying to tell you what to believe. I'm simply presenting an idea and allowing you to use your common sense Christianity to decide for yourself. Maybe every choice we've ever made, that can be viewed as either good or bad, is simply a decision to survive the moment as best we can. Now that my children are grown and feel more open to communicating freely, they inform me of things I did while raising them that hurt them and I am sometimes in absolute shock because in my mind I was helping them to succeed in life with loving and pure intentions but they felt wounded by my actions. I was the villain in their eyes and a hero in mine. Again, If God is everywhere in light and love, how can true darkness or evil really exist?

Chapter Twenty-One

DEMONS OF ANXIETY & DEPRESSION

I'm neither a doctor, nor a psychiatrist, so I encourage you upfront to pray about what I say and maybe even talk to a professional and decide for yourself. I struggled with anxiety and depression for many years and it almost killed me. I was able to get free from them and to help others get free as well. It was some of those other people who encouraged me to talk about this. I hope that I'm able to help you defeat anxiety and depression as well. Check out this scene from a Gospel Play I wrote many years ago Called, "Tricks of the Enemy". I toned the scene down some for this book but I caution you, this scene can be triggering.

In this short scene, the Devil is talking to a Young Man who is in the throes of depression.

The Devil speaking:

Poor Craig. Remember the other day at the gym and you asked that Pretty Girl for her phone number? Remember how she yelled out loud so everyone could hear her, "Get away from me"? Oh wow, Craig, that was embarrassing, wasn't it? But I mean you brought that on yourself. You knew you weren't on her level. Why would you even try to talk to her? Just keeping it real with you, Craig. You know you are worthless buddy. Hey, honestly you shouldn't be shocked even your grandma told you that you were never going to be nothing in life. She said that's why you bite your nails, remember? Oh yeah, that reminds me of something. Remember when you were in elementary school and you had diarrhea and you just couldn't make it to the bathroom on time, so Boo Boo ran all down your legs at school? What was that nickname the other kids were calling you? Oh, I remember, The Dookie King! LOL. You know I couldn't let you forget about that, because (singing) "That's what friends are for ". I'm your buddy Craig and I always got your back. So you know I'm gone, always keep it real with you Homey. The truth is you don't ever do anything right. You are worthless! Come on, you know you're a horrible parent. You ruined your kids' lives. You know you're a failure in life. You are still a little light-skinned idiot, just like your Stepdad said you were. The world will be better off without you, Craig. Kill yourself…

I apologize in advance that I may be a bit repetitive in this Chapter only because this is a very sensitive, very personal, and important message I want to share with you. Demonic Anxiety and Depression tormented me and almost killed me repeatedly. Although I no longer struggle with Depression or suicidal thoughts, I have still wrestled with Anxiety over the years. One major reason for that was because, for a long time, I assumed they were the same thing. Allow me to give a simple explanation of them both. Anxiety is worrying about something that may go wrong or any uncertain outcome. There can also be a constant uneasy feeling about the future with anxiety. Depression is feelings of despondency, dejection, and misery. At the height of my depression and suicidal thoughts. All it would take is one negative thought to come to mind. Then I would start to dwell on that thought and sooner or later, a bunch of other negative thoughts would just pile on top of that one. In no time flat, I would begin to feel like my life was useless and I should just kill myself. Then one day I heard my pastor say that the Devil comes to us and gives us bad thoughts and that they are not our thoughts, but they are the Devil giving us these bad thoughts. So I thought, it's not me! That liberated me a lot and at least it helped me get away from trying to kill myself. Because it gave me an adversary to focus on and to blame. While I was fighting with the Devil, I wasn't able to focus on my anxiety or my depression. I had an enemy to focus on. I'd be in Spiritual Warfare, talking in tongues, binding, and losing, tearing down strongholds, etcetera till I was exhausted. It was a release for me. For many years, when I would go into deep depression or anxiety, I would immediately go into spiritual warfare with the Devil and that would bring me out of my funk.

But it was always temporary. The Devil will always come back. Then I would be full of anxiety and depression all over again. Then one day Second Corinthians Chapter Ten, verse Five jumped out at me. It talked about "Casting down every imagination and high thought that goes against what God says about us. And bringing every thought into the obedience of Christ". That Scripture gave me strength and I felt for the first time that maybe I could control this. So I began to quote it as often as I could remember too. I would share it with other people until it became a part of my thinking. Then I began to see other verses that complemented the first one like Philippians Four and Eight which said, "Fix your thoughts on what is true. Honorable and pure. Whatever is lovely, good, honorable, whatever is of good report, if there is any virtue. If there is anything praiseworthy, think on these and meditate on these". I began to notice my life changing right before my eyes as my faith in these verses grew, so did my freedom. In the skit, you read at the beginning of this Chapter. Did you notice how the Devil talks to us just like we talk to ourselves? Maybe that's because it is us talking to ourselves or our minds talking to our souls. I now believe that my mind was just giving me more of what it believed I wanted. I was constantly thinking negative thoughts so my mind gave me more of what it assumed I wanted. What I was focusing on. Devil means accuser. Satan means adversary. Maybe I was my own accuser and adversary. We can choose to see the cup half full as opposed to half empty. Our minds are our servants and they serve us by helping us acquire the things that we focus on good or bad. Our minds don't judge our thoughts, they just bring us what we focus on. So choose to focus on positive thoughts. This isn't coming from Second William Chapter 2. I'm giving the Bible to prove these points. There are a lot of Scriptures that support this. Let me give you some more. "Believe that you received it and you shall have it". "Speak those things that be not as though they were already". "You shall have what you say". Finally, I'll submit, "Be it unto you, according to your faith". All of those Scriptures confirm that when you speak negatively or positively you will have it. When you believe in something good or bad you will receive it. Whatever you are focusing on, that is what you are going to get. Good or bad it is up to us. It wasn't until I realized that it was me causing those thoughts. That I was truly able to break free from depression. Once I realized that I could fix these issues myself, my life completely changed and yours can too. The late Pastor Reginald Lane in Detroit used to say, "You never get what you desire, you only get what you focus on". At the time I didn't understand all the wisdom that he was sharing, but now I truly get what he was talking about. We may desire or want certain things, but we only get what we focus on or what we place our attention on continually. If this is correct then we should focus on Joy, Peace, Health, Prosperity, and Love. Let's have gratitude for even the small good things in our life.

A lot of us think that repenting means. To cry out to God for forgiveness, but that's not what it means. The Greek word for Repent is Metanoia. It means to change your mind or a change of mind. The prevalent idea is to transform your thinking. The words repent, repentance, or repented are mentioned over 100 times in the Bible. That shows you how much and how important it is to change our way of thinking. I know this is a touchy subject and I am not a professional so let me give you more Scriptures that confirm this idea. "Faith is the substance of things hoped for, and the evidence of things not seen". Evidence for good or bad things, It's up to us. "As a man thinks, in his heart, so is he". Good or bad thoughts. There's a Scripture that says, "Cast your cares upon him". Cast means to throw and cares mean worries, so we are to throw our worries to God. God won't take your worries from you, but he will receive them from you. If you give them to him. He doesn't want you to be gentle and nice about it, he said, throw them to Him. The same urgency with casting down every negative thought, he tells us to get rid of them, to throw them away from us with force. The last one is "Be transformed by the renewing of your mind". In other words, change the way you think and your life will be changed. Again, this is not Second William Chapter Two. This is the Bible. Change your thoughts inside and it will change your world outside. A lot of times we pray for God to fix things for us. But he has already given us the ability and free will to fix them for ourselves. Remember Noah? God didn't deliver Noah and his family from the flood. He told Noah to go build this boat, go get you some nails, some hammers, and some wood or whatever, and you build this boat so you and your family will survive. Did God magically take His hands from Heaven and scoop Noah and his family up over the waters? Maybe they could see through the small separation in God's fingers, so they could see the waters covering the whole earth. Then maybe God said, "See how I have delivered thee and thy family, Noah". I think we view it that way but that is not what happened according to the Bible. God said you go build the boat then you and your family will be saved. Maybe that's the same thing He's telling us today. He said He has given us Dominion. He has given us free will, the ability to cast down our thoughts, to change our minds, to repent, and He instructs us to do it. I don't believe God would tell us to do something if He did not give us the ability to do it. But imagine if God did just reach into our minds or our hearts, and delivered us. The problem with that would be, that because we never changed our minds, we would simply just bring those negative thoughts that cause anxiety and depression right back to us. We have to change our minds to keep those things away from our lives. God would do us an injustice by coming down and fixing it for us once just to find us in the same or a worse state of being later. The best thing He could do is what He did. He equipped you to fix it yourself. You cast down those harmful thoughts. You throw those negative thoughts away, repent, turn away from bad thoughts, and think a different way. The Bible says that we reap what we sow. So if we are planting sad memories or sad thoughts. We will reap sad memories and sad thoughts. If we plant or if we sow good memories and good thoughts, we will reap good memories and good thoughts. Is it possible that reaping is not biased? Maybe the reaping process doesn't decide to only give us good? Maybe it will give us good or bad depending on what we choose to plant in our minds. Aren't we the ones who plant in our gardens? If we plant worries and fears of the future, we will reap more worries and fears of the future. That's the epitome of anxiety. If you want a harvest of love. Joy, peace, success then you have to plant those kinds of seeds. We have all the power. Please allow me to give you a few positive affirmation Scriptures that you should probably try to repeat as often as you can. Write them down on something, put them on your dashboard or your cell phone. Say these verses over and over again till you can feel them strengthen you. Please feel free to use any of the verses I've already mentioned in this Chapter. It is not the verses of scripture or the words of affirmation that heal you. It is your feelings and belief in those words or scriptures that change your life. These are powerful. I quote these daily. "No weapon formed against me shall prosper". Another one is "I am more than a conqueror through Christ Jesus." "I am an overcomer through Christ Jesus". I believe that even if you just start saying those right now, you could instantly begin feeling better. I feel better as I'm typing them. "Nothing shall by any means hurt me". Lastly my favorite, I say this every day, all day. "All things work together for my good". That means, no matter what happens, what's going on right now, even if I'm currently in the middle of something negative, I immediately say all things work together for my good, even this right now. Whatever it is, works for my good, my past mistakes, my failures, everything, all my shortcomings that would have me depressed and sad will work out for my good. The wrong ways I raised my kids, the things that I didn't do well enough, my being a bad husband, not being where I want to be financially, all my mistakes in life will work out for my good. I promise you that Life continually proves that to me and will do the same for you if you focus your mind on it. All those things that would cause you anxiety, depression, and sad memories turn around and bless you. That is the epitome of having the last laugh at the Devil and in Life. If bad thinking has a snowball

162

effect and amplifies throughout the day, piling on more and more negative thoughts, and more and more negative experiences then shouldn't it be the same, in reverse? Let me say it is the same in reverse. If you start your day off positively with positive thoughts, positive imaginations, and consciously thinking positively, a snowball effect happens, in the positive. More positive thoughts will come, and more positive experiences throughout your day. Start your day off thinking positively. Start by being grateful for everything good in your life, big or little. Be grateful that you've made it to see a brand new day. Be grateful that you can stand and walk. Be grateful that you slept in a bed as opposed to a cardboard box under a bridge. Even if you did sleep in a cardboard box last night. Be grateful that at least you had a cardboard box to sleep in to keep the elements off of you. Happiness is a choice. Choose to think positively, find things to be grateful for, and watch your thoughts begin to snowball throughout the day, in that same direction. You control this. It doesn't control you. Anxiety and depression cannot survive under those circumstances. Put anxiety and depression in an atmosphere they cannot breathe in and suffocate them. It's time to kill those negative thoughts. God has given us all we need to be successful against depression and anxiety. My life story reads like two different Williams. I contemplated suicide continually in my teens, I had a horrible temper most of my life but now people can't even believe me when I tell them that. They think I'm lying or exaggerating, and I love that. I changed my mindset to become this new and better version of William and I've still got a long way to go, but I'm nothing like I used to be. Changing my words and mind was like lifting weights in the gym. It was a struggle at first. I could only speak positive things with no belief or feeling. I had very little faith like the Bible says, a grain of mustard seed. I was hoping that more faith would come but until it arrived, I just kept crawling towards freedom in my mind. When I first went to the gym and started lifting weights, I could only get a 15-pound weight and maybe curl it one or two times then I had to put it down. But the more I kept going back to that weight, eventually I could get it up, 10 times then 15, and even 20 times. Then eventually 15 wasn't enough for me. I had to go get a 20lbs weight, then a 30-pound etcetera. I realized that my mental muscles were the same way. I can only mentally curl a little bit at first, but the more I keep pressing the weight, the easier it becomes, and the more things I could change in my life. The more I could press the weight of saying and thinking joyful, peaceful, and good thoughts, the easier it became. You are a creator, just like your Father God and you create the world around you. We are only slaves to our thoughts and emotions because we have allowed ourselves to be slaves to them. But we always could focus on them or change them, to whatever we want them to be. Whatever muscles we use the most will be the strongest. Which muscle are you going to use, negativity or positivity? It's up to you. The Bible says the truth shall make you free. You have just been given the truth. You are now free from anxiety and depression, the choice is yours when you are thinking good thoughts, you feel good and when you're thinking bad thoughts, you feel bad and full of anxiety, depression, and sadness. I promise you that you can feel some relief almost immediately. That happened to me and that's what helped my faith to grow because it didn't change my whole life overnight. But in those moments of saying some of those positive things about myself, I felt glimpses of peace, glimpses of joy, glimpses of release. It was almost like a drug. It just made me want more. Sometimes it was tough and I really didn't feel anything but you just have to keep pushing through. Again, just like in the gym, sometimes in the gym you're working out, you don't see any change. You're working out, you're crunching and you don't see anything but you keep doing it. One day you're going to look up and now you got a 6 pack. If you continue, thinking positive thoughts, they will eventually become second nature to you, just like your anxiety, depression and negative thoughts are second nature to you right now. Freedom is yours right now, but you have to seize it. I challenge you to try it and see for yourself. I pray this was helpful.

Chapter Twenty-Two

DEMONIC MINDSET

One day, I was on my way to the barbershop to get a haircut. Because the next morning I had an audition and right after the audition, I had a film shoot that I had to be at. On my way to the barbershop, my car cut off on me while driving. I was eventually able to get it started up, I then drove it to the mechanic, and he fixed something, I drove away and everything seemed fine. Then about 20 minutes later, It broke down on me, again. Once more, I was able to get it started and I made it back to the mechanic. He did something else to the car. We thought it was good. I drove away again on my way to the Barber, this time I got much further away from the mechanic, and all of a sudden the car broke down yet again, but after this breakdown, I could not get it started again. I had been optimistic all this time but now I'm beginning to break down like my car is. This is the third time on the same day. Anxiety is rising fast in my mind, what if the mechanic can't figure out what the problem is? He already tried to fix it twice. He thought it was fixed. It wasn't. I've already spent money on getting it fixed. Now I have to think about paying a tow truck to get it back to the mechanic. I'm worried about getting it back there before he closes as well as debating going to another mechanic since he could fix the problem twice already but I had already spent a bunch of money on him today as it was so why start from scratch elsewhere? Then it occurs to me that it's the 1st of the month, so the rent is due. I have to be careful with my spending. I go over all my options. I need to get a haircut because my hair is in bad shape and I've got an audition in the morning and I'm In a film shoot right after that. My thoughts are all over the place. At that moment, Worry, Stress, and Anxiety were running rampant in my head. I'm in the car, it's getting colder and colder because the car is not on and it's winter in Chicago, so I'm freezing sitting in this car trying to figure out what to do. I'm contemplating, if I pay for a tow truck will they come in time to get me to the mechanic today and if so will I even have enough money to get it fixed? Also, will my mechanic be able to figure out the problem today or at all since he has already failed twice today? My Anxiety was gaining momentum like a ball rolling downhill. Then I remember, Darn it, this upcoming weekend I've got to travel to Ypsilanti, MI to speak at a men's conference. My first Public Speaking Event where I was the Keynote speaker. I had been extremely excited about that. I panicked, will I even be able to make it, will I have to cancel my first speaking engagement? All this is happening to me. I'm trying to figure everything out. Going over everything repeatedly, shivering cold and overrun with worry. If I pay for the tow truck then would I have enough money to get the car fixed and be able to still pay my rent? Then what if I can't get the car fixed? What if I don't have enough money, what if the mechanic can't figure out what the problem is? My mind is just cluttered with stuff, so while I'm sitting in this car trying to figure all this out. Feeling overwhelmed, I got a phone call from my Supervisor from the job on the TV show Empire. He calls and says, "William, something happened today on set and I want to just give you a heads up. I apologize but You no longer have a job. Sorry about that, but you can go ahead and try to find employment somewhere else. Now it wasn't anything bad I did. In case you are wondering, something else happened with somebody else at the job, and that affected my job. So, I'm sitting in this freezing car. All of these incidents hit me at one time. Now my natural and immediate response because of years of religious programming was, Oh My God, the Devil was coming against me. He is attacking me, trying to destroy me. What did I do to cause all of this? Thoughts of spiritual warfare, binding and loosing, rebuking demons, and calling on God for help flooded my mind, but I could feel in my spirit that I was on the wrong track. Then in the midst of my panic-filled episode. I shook myself, took a deep breath, and tried to calm myself down. After a few calming breaths, I remembered, wait a minute the Devil has had no say so in my life for at least 10 years! I started speaking positively into my life, I started saying things like no weapon formed against me, shall prosper. All things work together for my good. Even in this situation, right now. I'm not worried about it. Everything's going to work out for my good. I don't know how and I'm not concerned about how. All things work together for my good. I didn't pray. I didn't ask God to help me, I didn't bind the Devil. I didn't speak in tongues nor did I go into Spiritual Warfare. I just spoke to the situation. I said everything works together for my good. I have no concerns. I am at peace. I am full of joy. I am prosperous, I am healthy, I am wealthy. After doing this for a few minutes. Just all of a sudden I felt optimistic again. I just felt good. I just didn't care how bad things looked. I was in the same situation. I still didn't have a job. I still didn't have my car working. I'm still getting colder by the minute. My mind felt free, even though I still had no solutions. It occurred to me to try to start the car again so I did and it started right up on the first try. I took it back to the mechanic, he fixed it that day for good. I was able to get everything taken care of. I got a Haircut, made it to the Audition, and made the Film shoot. I made it to my Speaking event and I got my Empire job back the next day. I could have stayed in that moment, brought the Devil back alive in my life, thinking Oh my God he got me. I could have given him that power back and then no telling how many other things he could have affected after that. Whenever anything negative happens in my life I stand still and speak positively. I only speak to the situation. I don't talk to the Devil, he's irrelevant. Things work together for my good even this, and nothing shall by any means hurt me. No weapons formed against me shall prosper. I am blessed wherever I go, wherever I am and whatever I put my hands to is prosperous and successful. I am Abundant. I am healthy, wealthy, and Wise. Scripture says, "Be it unto you according to your faith" and "Speak those things that be not as though they are". "Let the weak say, I am strong, let the poor say I am rich". Maybe we simply have a demonic Mindset? Maybe we are more in charge of our lives than we imagined. The Bible says that a prince when he is a child is no different than a servant, it isn't until he matures and inherits the kingdom that he becomes ruler of all. Maybe we are still stuck in servant mode, still behaving as children, crying out for God to save us when He has already gifted us with the keys to the kingdom. Maybe we are not truly victims, we simply just act like we are but the truth is we are Kings and queens, who have been according to Scripture given dominion.

Chapter Twenty-Three

THANK YOU, DEVIL.

I came from a fanatically religious background. I, along with almost every person I knew, believed I would be in Full Time Ministry one day. So in 2016 when I left Detroit and moved to Chicago to be a Stand-in and Photo double for the Actor Terrence Howard on the hit TV show, "Empire", several Christian friends were saying to me, "Don't get too excited because the Devil can bless you too. God wouldn't bless you to be on an unGodly show like Empire." This sentiment was amplified after I announced I had received an on-camera speaking role on season 5 of the show. I got messages and calls like, my Brother Please, don't let the Devil get you swept up in that Hollywood Hell, especially on a show that supports homosexuality, etc. Honestly, I wasn't upset at these messages because living in that religious mindset myself for decades, I completely understood where they were coming from. Honestly, I had given that same message to others in the past. With that said, having matured to a clearer, less religious viewpoint of Christianity, I am supposed to believe that the Devil blessed me and got me a job on a hit TV show, a job that I'm excited about going to every day, surrounded by people who bring me peace, joy, and excitement? Wow! Thank you, Devil. You're so sweet. LOL. As I've mentioned in earlier chapters I no longer view the devil as any kind of threat to my life in any way. Maybe I've been deceived? If that's true and if the Devil has been tricking me for over 10 years now, by no longer frightening me, no longer physically attacking me, smacking me in the face, knocking me off the couch, holding me down. Holding my mouth, holding my breath so I couldn't breathe, I no longer feel like evil spirits are choking me to kill me. If he is tricking me, by no longer haunting me like that. Thank you, Devil. Honestly, I appreciate it. Please continue tricking me into not being afraid of the dark anymore. I'm no longer afraid of being around people with bad spirits. I'm no longer afraid of any kind of demonic attacks. I no longer waste my prayer time binding demons and wrestling with the Devil. I can just simply talk to God and have great communication and conversations and learn and get more knowledge. I am free of fear to do those videos on my YouTube, setting people free, I can write this book without fear of demonic repercussions or attacks and setting more people free because of it. I personally believe my prayer time, my relationship with God and my mental state drastically improved once the Devil was removed from the equation. I was able to learn more about God, have a better understanding of God, and have a better relationship. If my friend's words of caution are true, that I'm being duped by the Devil, then I have to say I truly applaud Satan for helping me get closer to God and loving myself. Now I know some of you gasped when you heard me say thank you Devil but relax I'm being sarcastic. I know that no evil spirit has anything to do with my life period, not anymore. I'm going to tell you this. This book has planted a seed in you and as this seed grows, you will begin to fear the Devil less and less, you will begin to see him for what he really is. You will be less and less concerned about the Devil and his demons and their effect on your life, so you might not think that right now, but trust me, these seeds will grow. You will realize the truth, that the Devil is absolutely nothing to be concerned about.

Someone I care about and a person I am convinced cares about me recently told me that the Devil is tricking me, that he is fooling me into believing that he is weak or powerless so that he can destroy my life while I'm unprepared to defend myself. That reminded me of a quote I used to use against people who didn't believe in Satan. The quote is, "The Greatest Trick the Devil Ever Pulled Was Convincing the World He Didn't Exist!" I've never said that the Devil doesn't exist and neither am I saying he does exist, I am simply saying that he only has as much power over our lives as we believe he has. Even Jesus Christ is quoted in Scripture as saying, " Be it unto you according to your faith". My dear friend went on to caution me that the Devil wants me to believe that he doesn't have any real power to affect my life so that he can trick me and truly ruin my life without me being aware or fighting back. I know she cares about me, so I simply said thank you and respected her opinion. I didn't argue with her. I just decided it must be time to do a video about the Devil. So I did a series of videos on my YouTube channel called, "Us Crazy Christians", where I addressed a lot of things I mention in this book in a less detailed way, but using skits and humor to get my points across. The next chapter is from one of those videos.

Chapter Twenty-Four

ADAM - VS - JESUS

Back in early 2019, I recorded a video on my "Us Crazy Christians" YouTube channel titled "Adam vs Jesus '. It was a lighthearted debate between myself and a young man named Detroit Billie. I think the points made in this video can help people who struggle with the fear of losing themselves or their loved ones in the eternal damnation of hell. This chapter is a slightly amended transcript of that short video debate.

William

Welcome to Us Crazy Christians where we deal in common since Christianity I'm your host William Smith and today we're gonna have a battle to see who is greater Adam or Jesus. Joining me today all the way from Detroit Michigan let's give a warm welcome to

Detroit Billie. Praise the Lord Sir, what's going on Detroit Billie?

Detroit Billie
I'm doing well Bro. I'm ready to crack yo head in this debate.

William
Awesome, let's get into it, Detroit Billie. A few days ago you put a post on your Facebook saying that you believe that Adam is much more powerful and greater than Jesus. In that post, you also said that if you're correct that Adam is more powerful than Jesus then we should be followers of Adam and change our titles from Christians to Adamites.

Detroit Billie
No doubt homie. Adam is more powerful than The Temptations, Michael Jackson, Biggie, Tupac and Jesus all rolled together.

William
Huh!

Detroit Billie

No worries, homeboy, cuz I'm gonna prove it today. Better yet I'm gonna have you prove it for me.

William

I sincerely doubt that but please explain your argument to Me and Us Crazy Christians audience.

Detroit Billie

Ok. Let me ask you this. Why do you believe that Jesus is more powerful or greater than Adam?

William

Well, that's easy. Adam was just a man but Jesus is Christ the Messiah, The Anointed One, The Son of the Living God. Jesus is the Way, the Truth, and the Light. He is the Lamb of God. He is the Lion of the tribe of Judah, the Logos or the Word of God, the Light of the World, the Bread of Life. He is the Chosen One. I can keep going, He is our Lord and Master.

Detroit Billie

Master! Who's master? He yo master, ain't nobody my master. You can keep that to yourself, Bro. Anyway, you just gave me a lot of nice titles for Jesus but like the Prophetess Janet Jackson once said, "What have you done for me lately?" Come to think of it, I know several prophets, apostles, bishops, deacons, preachers, ministers, and pastors who have a good title in front of or behind their name but they don't do anything for anybody. Titles mean diddly. What has Jesus done in action to prove that He is better or more powerful than Adam?

William

Jesus did many miracles. He caused the blind to see, He healed the sick, and He raised the dead. Adam didn't do any of that.

Detroit Billie

True dat, true dat. But according to scripture many people in the Bible before Jesus and after Jesus did those same miracles. Who's to say Adam couldn't have done the same things if the opportunity arose? I mean after all according to the Bible it was the beginning of mankind, maybe nobody was blind or deaf back then. What's so special about Jesus besides all those nice titles he got?

William
Jesus laid down his life to set us free from the curse of sin and death.

Detroit Billie
Good, now we are talking. Who was the "us" you were just referring to in that statement?

William
His children, those who love him, follow him and accept him as Lord and Savior. Those who cry out to him. We confess our sins to him, believe in him, and trust in him.

Detroit Billie
Just so I'm clear in understanding you. Are you saying that if we do these things you stated then Jesus will set us free from the curse of sin and death right?

William

Absolutely. As a Christian I am set free from the curse of sin and spiritual death, right now.

Detroit Billie

How did sin enter the world?

William

Through Adam. Sin entered into the whole world through Adam's sin in the Garden of Eden. After he ate the forbidden fruit.

Detroit Billie

I wondered when we would get back to my main man Adam, the Master of the Universe. So you say, sin entered the world through Adam. Were you and I affected by Adam's actions?

William

Yes sir.

Detroit Billie

How many sins do we have to commit to become a sinner? One hundred sins, ten sins, or just one sin?

William

None, we were born into sin. This is why Jesus had to come down to earth and put on earthly flesh and….

Detroit Billie

Slow your roll play pimpin. I see you about to jump into preacher mode. Just answer the question big fella and save your sermons for Sunday. Thank you very much. Are you an Adamite? Meaning do you pray to Adam or read Adam's Bible? Do you serve Adam, follow Adam, or have faith in Adam?

William

Absolutely not!

Detroit Billie

Interesting. What about Hindus, Buddhists, Native Americans, and people in remote African villages or foreign lands who may have never heard of Adam? Since they don't know who Adam is, they obviously don't believe in or have faith in Adam either. Are they still born into sin because of Adam?

William

All mankind was born into sin. If they haven't accepted Jesus Christ as their personal Lord and Savior didn't....

Detroit Billie

Excuse me, Bro. There you go again. I don't see any offering plates, so I guess you don't need to be preaching right now. A simple yes or no is sufficient Reverend.

William

Yes.

Detroit Billie

Let me repeat what you said to me and the Us Crazy Christians audience. You said Jesus came to lay down his life to set his people free. His people are those who believe in Him, who serve Him and follow him, etc, etc... You also said, that we were all born into sin, every human on earth. All of mankind is affected by Adam's sin, even if we've never even heard of Adam.

William

That's right, yes.

Detroit Billie

Allow me to reiterate for clarity. Even if you have never heard of Adam, the world is still affected by Adam's choices. We obviously don't need to believe in Adam to be affected by what Adam did. But on the other hand, Jesus the Messiah is limited to only being able to affect those who believe in him. Interesting. My main man Adam, just simply ate a piece of fruit to affect and infect every person's life on the entire planet, past, present, and future! That's like I hauled off and smacked you dead in your mouth and everybody on Earth felt the pain of it. Then Jesus comes to fix or heal what I did and goes to apologize to the cities of Detroit, Flint, and Chicago but failed to make it to the rest of the planet. So let's look at this again. The only thing my man Adam did was take a bite out of an apple God told him to leave alone while your man Jesus gave His life, was beaten beyond recognition, suffered pain, abuse, degradation, was betrayed by His own people, and brutally murdered, etc… and after doing all of that He can only affect small a group of people who believe in him? I've also heard that even some of those who believe in Him could lose his favor and his salvation after they've already had faith in him. Wow, that doesn't seem like Jesus has that good of a handle on things. Come on William, just admit the truth, it's obvious that Jesus is weak compared to my main man Adam. Case closed playboy.

William

Jesus did come to save the whole world but Adam was a bully and forced his sin on us but Jesus is a gentleman and He asks us to join him if we want to. He is kind and gentle and won't force himself on us.

Detroit Billie

Now that's some bull, William. You know that's not even in Scripture. Preachers made that up to explain why Jesus seems so weak in comparison to Adam. I know you could come better than that baby boy. I'll wait.

William

(No response. Thinking)

Detroit Billie

Let me help you out before you end up making me late for my date tonight. John the Baptist said, "Behold the lamb that takes away the sins of the WORLD. In John chapter four it calls him "the savior of the WORLD". First Corinthians chapter fifteen says, "Just as in Adam, ALL of us died, so too in Christ ALL OF US, will be brought to life." Romans chapter five says, "just as one man sinned led to condemnation for ALL so by one man's act of righteousness led to justification for ALL." Down a little further it says because of what Jesus did, just how about sin dominated in death now grace has dominion through life so EVERYTHING we lost in Adam we have RECOVERED through Christ. In 1st Corinthians, Paul calls Jesus the second Adam and the last Adam sent from heaven. Paul explains that Jesus is the second Adam because he affects the WHOLE WORLD just like Adam did but to a greater degree and a much better end.

William, do you know what a legal precedent is?

William

Yes, I do. A legal precedent or a legal authority is a legal case that establishes a principle or rule of law. This is used when deciding later cases with similar issues or facts.

Detroit Billie

Good job. Bout time you got something right. Anyway, a biblical president was established when one man Adam sin entered the world and affected all mankind. Likewise, when Jesus set men free by his death on the cross, he set ALL men free. Not just those who believe in Him. If it works that way for Adam, it should be able to work that way for Jesus and even more so because after all Jesus is the second and much improved Adam as well as the Son of the Living God. If not then Adam is in fact more powerful and greater than Jesus, facts. Even the scriptures say that Jesus came to set the whole world free so why are so many of Us Crazy Christians overlooking that? William, was Jesus unsuccessful? In other words, William, is the son of God a failure? I'm gonna need you to use your common sense Christianity to figure that one out homeboy cause I gotta go. I got a hot date with a little light-skinned honey from Vegas, Playboy. So I'm about to be out, deuces.

William

Thank you, Detroit Billie. His last question really grabbed me. "Was Jesus a failure? According to the Bible, His goal was to save the whole world. Did Jesus fumble the bag? Maybe we just misunderstood the scriptures on this subject of salvation. Now that I think of it John 3:16 says, God so loved the World that He gave His Son Jesus, meaning even God wanted to save the world. Does that mean that both God and Jesus are failures? I remember a young lady messaged me and asked me a question about working on the TV show Empire some years ago. I immediately answered her question and forgot about it. But years later I ran into this young lady and she said to me, "You never answered my question about working on Empire." I said, "Yes I did, look at your messenger." She pulled it up right in front of me and saw that I had given her an answer years ago, but for some reason, she never noticed my response. The point is that although she didn't realize that she had the answer, the fact is, it was hers nonetheless. She had it for years, she just didn't know it. But as soon as she came face-to-face with me, the answer giver, I confirmed the fact that she was unaware of it. The truth was that she had already received the answer. I simply exposed her to a truth that she was ignorant of. Ignorance of a fact does not negate the fact. Is it possible that Jesus was very successful and that we and the rest of the planet are saved and always have been saved, but we just didn't know it? If Jesus is greater and more powerful than Adam and if Jesus and God were successful in their mission then maybe you will see your unsaved uncle again in heaven. Maybe you will see your brother that never became a Christian but you loved him and you prayed for him for years. Maybe he's with God right now waiting to see you again. Maybe your unsaved Parent or your unsaved Child is in heaven with God as happy and

194

peaceful as can be just waiting to see you again. Maybe your unsaved best friend or cousin didn't realize that Christ died for them so they didn't walk in that knowledge during this lifetime but maybe as soon as they came face to face with the answer Giver He told them the truth. That he died to save the whole world and that included them. He had already successfully solved all of their issues and problems but they just didn't know it and maybe you will see your loved ones again in peace and joy in heaven even though they never said the sinner's prayer. Even though you may have learned a lot of doctrine that led you to believe the opposite of what I'm saying, I am sure that your spirit knows this to be true. The peace and joy that rose in your heart as you read that is evidence of its validity.

Detroit Billie set me up, he set us all up, but I'm still processing it all. What do you think? Are Jesus and God horrible failures or have they succeeded in saving the world as planned?

In 2 Peter 3:9 (NIV) God is recorded as saying, The Lord is not slow in keeping his promise, as some understand slowness. Instead, he is patient with you, not wanting anyone to perish, but everyone to come to repentance.

In Isaiah 46:10 (AMP) God says, "Declaring the end *and* the result from the beginning, And from ancient times the things which have not [yet] been done, Saying, 'My purpose will be established, And I will do all that pleases Me *and* fulfills My purpose,'" The same verse in the New International Version of the Bible reads, "I make known the end from the beginning, from ancient times, what is still to come. I say, 'My purpose will stand, and I will do all that I please.'" To paraphrase God said in 2 Peter that His will is to save everyone and Isaiah it states that God's purpose, His good pleasure or His Will (depending on which translation you read) is that all come to repentance and He will accomplish His Will. Love never fails and God is Love so He never fails either.

Chapter Twenty-Five

EVIL - VS - YOU

Maybe we shouldn't take the Bible so literally. Consider that Judaism did not have a satan in their theology till nearly Chronicles and they believed that everything that happened on the Earth, good, bad, mass destruction, etc, was all from God. So if an earthquake happened they would say God opened the Earth and killed folks. So when we read the bible we must understand that it was written by individuals who were polytheistic, largely superstitious, who believed the Sun revolved around the Earth and it was flat. Many of them were writing about how they viewed God as opposed to how God truly is. Maybe the bible writers were mere men just like us with the same insecurities, flaws, misunderstandings, prejudices, and imaginations. I want to take you back for a moment to remember the beginning of my story of "My Time With The Devil." Remember before I saw the movie, "The Exorcist". Before my mom told me about demons and what they could do to me and what they did to her and I got all this confirmation from my Uncles and Aunties. Before receiving and eventually believing this information, I was never afraid of demons. I wasn't afraid of the dark. I could sleep without a night light, without the lights on. I wasn't afraid of bumps in the night. I mean, if I heard something I might have thought it was a person. I mean, we were in a bad neighborhood and sometimes people would break into the house even when we were home because people knew it was only my little brother and I under the protection of our young, pretty mother. So, there was a fear of that. But as far as a fear of demons, ghosts, and the Devil, they were irrelevant to me. They didn't affect my life. They didn't take up any of my mind time. But as soon as I was convinced that the Devil was real, that he was powerful, that he could do all these things to me, that he could torment me, that he could choke me, and that he could possess me like he did the girl in, "The Exorcist". All of a sudden he became powerful in my life, all of a sudden he could do these frightening things because again, the Bible says, "Be it unto you according to your faith". If you believe it, it is so. As soon as I began to change my mind and my beliefs about the Devil through God telling me that these things happened to that woman because she believed it. Then after I started doing the Devil character in my play and began visualizing him as weaker and weaker, he just simply became weaker and weaker in my mind and life. To the point right now, where he is truly nonexistent. I don't even think about him until somebody else brings him up. Could our minds function just like a computer and simply do as it is programmed? I believe our minds can create things for us. Good or bad. Whatever we focus on, whatever we have faith in, whatever we put stock in. Good or bad, our minds are not prejudiced or swayed toward one way or the other. It just gives us what we focus on, what we think about what we believe, be it unto us, according to our faith. "You shall have whatever you say", the Bible says. If my mind, my thoughts, or my beliefs can manifest all these horrible things that I went through for over 30 years wrestling with the Devil. Painful attacks, physically being hit, just crazy supernatural things happening often. What if I consciously focused my same beliefs, my same thoughts, my same mind, my same focus, and put it towards good things, towards powerful things? What if I focused on believing what God can do, what Jesus can do, what I can do? Our minds are not prejudiced. It's not just giving us bad things. It's giving us what we believe, what we focus on, what we see, and what we think is possible. A good example is the four-minute mile. There was a time when no one could ever do it. It was believed to be impossible. It was a widespread belief that a human running that fast would cause their hearts to explode. Until someone did it. One person didn't believe it was impossible. When he didn't believe it, he was able to do it, and once he did it, several other people did it in that same year, because now it's believed it could be done. Our minds can create so many things for us. Good or bad, even miraculous, it's up to us to decide.

Please be patient with me. I know that this Chapter is a little repetitive but I really want to drive this point home.

What if we used our minds or our imagination to think wonderful things, to imagine wonderful things? What if we thought of ourselves as powerful, healthy, wealthy, wise, full of love, joy, peace, and compassion? What if we saw ourselves that way? What if we visualized that? What if we believed that about ourselves? If we can create things in the negative, likewise, we can create things in the positive. Our Father God is the creator and we are His children. Is it possible that we can create just like him? I think we create or manifest the world around us and how it affects us. Examine your life. Is your world good or bad? Maybe that's up to us. Do demons run your life? Maybe that's up to us. If you believe God is good, then He is. If you believe God is vindictive, then He is. If you believe God is moody, then He is. If you believe God is kind, compassionate, loving, and caring, then He is. What do you believe? What do you believe about God? What do you believe about the Devil? Be it unto You, according to what you believe. Now let me clarify, God is good all the time and our beliefs about Him can't make Him bad. But our beliefs can blind us to the truth and cause us to see things the wrong way. Just like you can have water in a glass halfway and you can see that glass as half empty or you can see that glass as half full. The choice is ours but that choice doesn't change the amount of water in it, but it does change how you view that water. Whether you're happy about that water or sad about the amount of water, doesn't affect the amount of water, so simply choose to see it half full. Can it be that simple? Scripture says, "God's way is so simple a fool can not miss it". So let me ask you how powerful is the Devil in your life? It's up to you. I hope this book blesses you and sets you and your loved ones free from the fear of Hell, The Devil, and all Evil spirits' control in your life. Be Blessed.